To:

with Love
&
I hope you
enjoy the
poems

From: Paul x

Introduction.

Welcome, everyone, to my third book on Scottish Independence.

I would like to thank everyone who has contributed to this book and by that I mean all of you who have supported and encouraged me to keep writing, even in the most difficult times. The names are far too many to mention as they are thousands in number. We were strangers when we met but are now friends, some are my best friends now. There are those I do not like, some I will never forgive for what they have done but, ultimately, I would not change it for anything.

I had no vote in the last Independence Referendum in 2014 as I was living was just outside London then but I am home now, back in sunny Yoker, where I was born.

I would like to thank one person in particular for "doing my flitting". A lot of The YES Movement know David McGuinness and I still owe him for this. I was due to move up to Glasgow from west London, Isleworth, on 30th June 2017 but my brother wasn't well enough to drive down and back up. Without knowing this, and minutes later, David sent me a message asking if I had someone to drive me "back up the road". I told him what had happened and he said he couldn't do it that weekend but would do it the following weekend. I booked the earliest flight for that Saturday morning, met David at Heathrow, hired a van and headed to my house in Isleworth for the last time. We loaded up the 20' truck with whatever I was taking along with 90 boxes and set off for Glasgow. We got to Glasgow, Yoker, and unloaded the truck and were completely knackered after trudging up the stairs to the third floor tenement. Apart from a few coffee break stops, there was no real break and David would not take a penny for all his work. I have to thank Sarah, lovingly known as The Dragon, too who went a whole day without seeing her husband. She later thanked me for that! Thank you both for everything. x

The artwork on this cover is by someone who is already a legend in the Yes Campaign and I cannot praise this man's excellent work enough. I had the very real privilege of having our own Indy artist and friend, Michael Larkin aka Wee Skribbles, adorn my last book with his fabulous artwork and he has very kindly given his permission for me to use "the strange horsey chess piece" on this book. No money exchanged hands but a deal was done! Thank you Michael and Fi. x

Now that I have a vote, I will be voting and YES. Some Unionists will say, we are anti-English but this is not about a person's place of birth but rather a case of self-determination, self-governance and, if "anti" anything, it is anti-Westminster. We have many organisers of our biggest rallies who are English, we even have English Scots for YES and lovely people they are too, I know I have met them on many various rallies. And how can I be anti-English when my son is?

We are almost at our journey's end and soon we will be leaving the United Kingdom and not before time either. I am sure the MSM will be wondering what will happen to them as they turned against their country at every, paid, opportunity. Where will the politicians go once we have set out our country, will the SNP disband and will the others, Unionist Parties, start to work for Scotland instead of against it? They will need to! The Green Party Members seem to be the only ones who are safe and have no need to change. That's my opinion anyway.

The Bill of Rights which was passed in Parliament, ensured that we, the people of Scotland, are sovereign and hold the power in our hands to take control of this beautiful country once again. On the 10th March 2019, David Davis confirmed this, when referring to Brexit, he said that no treaty existed whereby one partner cannot walk away. This was again reiterated by Geoffrey Cox as he addressed Parliament on Brexit, 12th March 2019. Aye, they're pretty useless and contradict themselves daily.

I hope you enjoy the poems.

Paul x

Foreword.

We are wrapped, not in chains or cotton wool but embalmed in a Union cloth that lets us breathe but just enough to stay alive. As we wriggle to escape, to enhance our standing and be free to engage in what is ours with the greater world or even that of our neighbours in Europe, we are annointed with the cheap smell of Westminster's perfume which we accept with a thanks and a bow into further submissive state. But the stale smell is always there from yesterday's splattering yet is hidden from today with our daily dose of their new aromatic benevolence. This cloth is what we are falsely bound to, as are their chains of state.

Our mouths and eyes are thinly veiled to let us see and hear just enough for a clouded view or muffled understanding of the orator's, our masters, meanings where truth cannot be exposed or allowed to penetrate. Our acceptance belittles our standing for we are not meant to understand. Our hands try to reach out but are loosely bound, hindering us whilst accommodating their wishes. We are fed a daily drip of hope but that is all it is, hope for they will never allow us the powers any normal country has. There is no hope of our voice being heard while we are tethered to Westminster's disproportionate political numeracy where 59 Scottish voices are scoffed at and voted down by 533 English MPs. Disproportionate, dysfunctional and an utter disgrace to democracy. Scots do not sit in London's banqueting halls, feasting like them nor receive invitations to talks that could enhance or rupture our land or her people but neither do we starve, we are alive and they ask our gracious thanks for this pitiful and forced existence we find ourselves going through. While they shoot grouse and deer and other game on stolen lands, they give us foodbanks to exist on, not to fill our bellies but to exist. That is all, to merely exist!

We are engulfed in corruption, sadly too often by our own, enveloped in a cloth that was made in Scotland with the dank smell of Westminster occasionally sprinkled over us to disguise the smell of our death but the cloth is old and rotting, its seams are frayed and worn and we are pushing through with withered hands. Our hearts are pumping fresh new blood daily, our minds have been alerted to the false promises and lies, the vows that never came to be and how we are being clad with the views of England to the point of mockery by a world of friends who now look on this pathetic union with the contempt it has always deserved. And they fear this.

Their wars are not ones we asked for but we are being dragged into them and these weapons of mass destruction that sit idly by, corroding and leaking their toxic poison into our waters are not what we want but what are forced upon us by Westminster. These nuclear submarines with their warheads lie just along the road from Glasgow, Scotland's biggest city and as Westminster admitted, they are a hazard to us all and are not a deterrent to war. The warheads are frequently replaced and driven through England and Scotland's country roads in convoys and they have a had a few near misses over the years. One error is the last they will make.

Our lands have seen enough desertion, mostly forced and thrown to the corners of an Empire they still believe exists and I am certain some are of a mind that it will come again! Our fertile lands which once housed thousands now lie derelict of our indigenous people, their houses burned down and, some, with the tenants still inside. Our people were replaced with sheep by the traitors to Scotland who bowed to the nobility at the command of those from another land. And were handsomely paid for it. We, the people of Scotland, are insignificant and always have been as it is only the wealth of our resources they require and will ultimately fight for. This will not be given up by the British state and it will not, now, be surrendered by the people of Scotland. Our insignificance to them will be their ultimate downfall as Scots now see the State for what it really is.

We have been divided by every means possible and they fear that one day we will unite. That day is almost here and they fear this.

Prior to the union, Westminster brought in The Alien Act in 1705 which shows how anxious England was for Scots' wealth. Scotland is a country and a nation as much as England is and we should not accept we are inferior to anyone. Yet not superior either. This Act of Union was signed in 1707 as countries of equals by the greedy of both nations with the greed of Scottish nobles held to ransom by the greed of the English with not a shred of loyalty to the people they represented. This was pure blackmail and failure to sign meant war.

We were not an impoverished nation asking England for help and when they mention "Darien", only Scotland's wealthy were affected by this by their investment and they failed only because the Dutch and English ships prevented Scotland from securing that trade route. Scotland was wealthy and has wealth now that most countries can only dream of but these riches are not shared equally throughout this disunited kingdom. They are held almost exclusively by the wealthy. We feather their beds for them whilst laying cardboard on our streets for the ever increasing dispossessed of our own.

The British establishment took our tongue for two hundred years, forbade the wearing of tartan and playing the bagpipe. This was punishable by imprisonment or shipped abroad to the Jamaicas or beyond. They have draped their union flag all over anything we hold dear, castles, churches etc. and now they are shoving it right in our face, plastered all over our foodstuffs in supermarkets. The MSM almost refuse point blank to cover any good deeds emanating from Holyrood yet feel obliged to thrust upon us every fault that is known to man, even those failings from outwith Scotland are deemed ours. They have asset stripped us all, England included, for centuries and rely on the poorest paving gold paths and mansions for these elitists who rule us. We will dwindle to nothing if we do not insist on running our own country and their contempt shows no signs of abating. It is down to us, no-one else. It is up to us!

Many have written much more eloquently than I over the past three hundred years of this union's existence and what I write is only a poor continuation of what they witnessed and went through. Indeed nothing has changed apart from the fact that Scotland is even more diminished now than it was then but it is within our grasp now to become the nation we once were.

Almost half of Scotland has been awake for some time with others joining us daily but when will England's people awaken to the injustice they have?

Paul x

Death by Tories.   **31.10.16.**

These grandest thieves love contraband

An' whit better prize than oor wee land

An' clypes will aye fa' roon' aboot

When threatened wi' the tackit boot!

They fa' intae the feebled mind

An' caring not, we're no' their kind

They bait wi' scant an' false remarks

Wi' hateful words an' mindless acts.

They'll condemn ye mair if auld or poor

While keepin' sentries at yer door

Let naeb'dy see whit fate awaits

As they then they charge wi' haste an' hate

An' these soulless bastards waste nae time

In stating death's a legal crime.

Like jackals, wolves, they have their feed

Then wash their hands when you are deid!

Their Democracy.   **12.5.17.**

What kind of soul has her god forged?

What bitterness it spills,

She mocks us through indifference

With the poorest, savaged, killed!

She speaks of her democracy

And purveys this for her dream

Gliding through unchallenged, she declares,

I am May, this is my team.

This woman has an appetite,

An insatiable thirst for power

And cares not how she gets it

As through those depths she'll scour

The power that swarms within that mind

Refutes all logic, others bear

But that defiancy will consume her

Within her toxic air.

Who Cares?   **25.5.17**

You think you are free but everyone's owned

You're only a servant of the state and a throne

And those paid to protect us now hide behind guns

They're now the protected and it's us who are shunned

And the older we get, the more sorrow we feel

As the State's deathly voice shouts and brings us to heel

Heads burst with emotions, we feel all the rage

But our memories tell us we've covered that page.

They silently watch us, we feel under threat

Like stern schoolmasters with no one their pet

We've to talk, we've to smile but we can't feel at ease

As our army patrols our streets now diseased.

It's all part of their plan, the Controllers are here

They've finished rehearsals now feel, see their fear

The guns here are loaded beneath bullet like stares

But who'll now hear our voices and who really cares?

For Kezia.   **27.5.17.**

How can the honest worker's wage

Stretch to cover all these gaps

It's eked then stretched and eked again

'Til all its strength is sapped,

Once we had a Party

Who fought to ease that pain

But today it's all too personal

As they live their lives for gain.

It's degenerative, immoral

It's your Scottish suicide

The Branch that once could weigh their votes

Is colluding with a side

A side they've always stood against

That enemy, the foe

Who do you stand against today?

I'm sure The Tories know

And just who have you united with

Those who instigate

Those callous cuts to Forces

To instil their own police state

They bring laws of self-destruction

Where the poorest bear the costs

The annihilation of our rights

Where humanity is quashed.

They are waiters hired to pick up scraps

And do it with great pride

They're just lackies being shafted

But it seems they love the ride,

Their fayre is more than bitter

But they dare not compromise

Disaster is their recipe

With their secrets lined with lies.

This is hatred served with bigotry

Dished up by The Union's crooks

With Britain First, The BNP,

The Orange Order on their books.

You lost your core allegiance

When you shared that Tory bed

And now you think you'll get it back

Did you not hear what we said?

Pumping Fear.   **28.5.17.**

While we search for the terror before us

Look not to some far distant shore

And don't tell me it's all down to ISIS

We fund them, we're at their core

Of course ISIS will say it's their doing

It's an advert to pump up their fear

But we reap what we sow in these countries

So don't look over there, look here.

Just who are the bombers, the terrorists

We've blown these countries apart

And for what? Gold, oil and fortunes

It is us who wear the black hearts.

Look at the states we have aided

Israel, Saudi et al

Then look what they do with their weapons

While the world turns away from it all.

If a terrorist's white and he's Christian

He's a god fearing lonely lost soul

But if he's brown and a Muslim, it's Islam

Some truths will never be told.

It's about division and conquer

Instilling a fear that they own

A fear they manipulate wisely

For a broken union and throne.

Nicola Sturgeon f.m.   **30.5.17**

Some aspire to greatness, some are thrust on us to serve

And sometimes, if you're lucky, you get what you deserve

She is never complacent, her vision is clear

And it's the will of the people that leads us to here.

Do you not wonder where we found one like this

Who talks freely to parents and their baby she'll kiss

She'll then stop, pose for selfies, hundred or more

She's the one who puts country and her folk to the fore.

She doesn't walk up and ask if she's allowed

She dives right in, freely, she's a part of the crowd

She's revered by a public, she's not some superstar

For up here in Scotland, you are who you are!

She speaks out with passion, like no other, with pride

And despite what "they" tell you she has Scots on her side

She fights from our corner for those in need most

Up here in Scotland, Oor Nicola's the toast.

She's tough, she's resilient, knows every move that you'll make

But if you think "Small" and "Woman", that's your biggest mistake

She's the heart of her people, they are with her, they're proud

And if you need reassurance take a look at her crowds.

She emulates pop stars with talks sold out in hours

There's a mutual love, we are hers, she is ours

It's her love of the people, this country, our land

She's the Queen of all Scotland by the people's command.

SCOTLAND'S DISASTER.   **31.5.17.**

It seems she's pronouncing, some laws of her own

But her voice from the wilds is an eerie-like drone

She talks of democracy but only when it suits her

Whilst snarling at the protests, like some mad, rabid cur.

Like Mother Theresa, the Westminster one,

She bays from the dark side then declares it's in fun,

Some here have told me she's a born and bred Scot

Some say North Korean but that's a bold, wishful thought.

If she's Kim Jong-un's sister then we're in for a ride

We'd best double up sentries in Faslane, on The Clyde

She could be threat but have you seen her plan

She wants to be Premier and destroy our wee land.

Why's she constantly attacking Holyrood's SNP?

She wants that red button, they want a land nuclear free

Yet her pictures go viral when she's out in her tank

And just like her brother she's, for now, firing blanks.

But she's started already with acts that are vile

She's proposing that breakfasts are stopped from each child

And she's watching the oldest, watching their dying breath

If they're cared for, their house, is hers on their death!

Is this woman normal, is this who you want?

A woman whose friends are The National Front

One who goads Fascists to take to our streets

While smiling for cameras look at me cute and sweet!

She's callous, she's heartless, she's headstrong, a fool

A woman, who believes, one day, she could possibly rule!

WM.   5.6.17.

Nae mair will we despise ye

Nae mair ye'll gie's yer hate

For come the day when we are free

We'll be oor ain true fate.

The Tories and The DUP.   12.7.17.

Museums closed, roads shut down for the Unionists'
Parade

Let's divide and conquer yet again with our bigoted tirade

In Scottish towns and cities even in our village squares

They lined along divided streets and displayed this summer's fayre

And in their ranks were Irish, singing the Irish must go home

Don't you know the famine's over, get back across the foam!

Theresa May discussed with a mob full of hate

A way forward, she tells us, that will make Britain Great

She's a whore to the system and doesn't care who she beds,

To her, power is all, and it's gone to her head.

That bright orange bigoted sash that she wears

 The one you all bow to but pretend it's not there,

Well look at her now, swathed in Orangemen's glee

And the party that wears it, is the Orange DUP.

Is peace in the Provinces now out of her hands,

And how can she be neutral when you bow to demands

From a party who denies its own people their rights

It's an Orange allegiance and the future's not bright!

In Belfast, old tyres, will belch out thick black smoke

And pallets draped with hated flags belies the hatred that it stokes

The Tories have brought back to us, the days all Ireland feared

It seems the saboteurs of peace have made their stance quite clear.

Why do governments allow them, sectarian marches such as these,

How can peace move forward when our streets are still diseased?

Power always has a price but you should never sell your soul

And never sell your people off with a pocketful of gold.

The Foe. 15.7.17.

I fought injustice, I fought in wars

But knew not what I was fighting for,

They gave me guns and said on you go

Then told me who was friend and foe.

I killed and killed and I killed again

As red blood ran from these foreign men

Then face to face, two you young men stood

Two frightened men, misunderstood.

I lunged, my bayonet pierced his chest

I watched him as he lay down to rest

He asked me why I was his foe

My answer was, I did not know.

Just a shepherd boy of sixteen years

He died with eyes that were filled with tears,

Why was I here, I had to know

But that young man here was not my foe.

It was their injustice, it was their war

Now I knew who I was fighting for

I returned my guns and said on you go

You are no friend, YOU are my foe.

The Apolitical Army.   23.7.17.

Go gather up your armies and lead them into war

You are the reason why they fight and it's you they're dying for

Fields of green are blackened by dead silhouettes of men

You bury them, the grass returns then send our soldiers in again!

How many lives must lovers lose before another falls

While you store up your riches and celebrate with some big ball?

You speak like you're victorious but there's nothing to rejoice

Tell the children that you left behind who want to hear that soldier's voice!

All they hear is suffering when you knock upon their door

Dressed up in your military with a letter from their corps

Your medals shine into their eyes as you tell them how they died

You tell the kids they're heroes and celebrate their death with pride.

The kids grow up believing this and when they're women, men

They go out and die for your cause and that door gets knocked again

Then a politician's interviewed sporting finest army dress

ENLIST, fight for your country, I'll control you from my desk!

This Unequal Measure.   26.7.17.

Now that Downing Street's banned our First Minister

From debating on what they have to say

There's no input from Scotland; No Scottish voice,

Aye! This Union, it seems, had its day.

No wonder the Scots feel repulsed

We're rejected by an undignified horde

A rabble of millionaire puppets

Who're aspiring to be Ladies or Lords

With no participation there should be no deliberation

If an equal is refused the right to speak

They once sought our alliance but now show defiance

Do they really think Scots are that weak?

They are the weakness, they are the diseased

They're the virus without any cure

Their ill thought out plans are just hapless demands

And the gauntlet still lies at their feet

They'll retire to bed, wake up scratch their head

Each day's just a mundane repeat!

They hear but don't listen to what's being said

This ensemble are worse than a farce

They offered us hope but instead gave us rope

Whilst kissing this Premier's arse.

These indignant, pompous, arrogant fools

Have no honour, dignity, guile

They're repugnant, discourteous, don't share a brain

And handpicked by a woman so vile.

This incredulous cretin who listens to none

Negates every promise she makes

If it's chaos you want with sectarian taunts

This woman has got what it takes!

Less than three years ago, they pleaded don't go

Scotland can lead from the front

Now we're cast to the wind, the vow has been binned

And our First Minister is now an affront!

Spine.   3.8.17.

They act out their scene to the sound of their voice

With each phrase delivered to an elegant poise

It's all perfectly angled, it's their portrayal of you

All their thoughts reflected and all their points of view.

Your world is one of acceptance and you, very seldom, ask why

You believe what these people tell you yet know their truths are all lies.

What happened to that spine you had was it politically removed?

For no matter what they tell, your ignorance always approves!

Aye! You'll curse these bastards; who the fuck do they think they are?

But in the end, you just accept it and applaud all the lies of these stars.

Look beyond their media and read up on the facts

And that spine, you thought you'd lost, you'll find you've got it back!

The Betrayal and Death of William Wallace.
3 .8.17.

The pact was signed in Rutherglen's Kirk where a name would be revealed

Just another Scotsman's life betrayed, another Scot whose fate was sealed

He was captured at Robroyston by a Lord, Sir John Menteith

And the Guardian of all Scotland, no more her air he'd breathe.

In silence they dispatched the news, their riders swiftly raced

To alert King Edward Longshanks, that The Wallace was disgraced

For three long weeks, bound hands and feet, they paraded England's prize

Though anger raged within his heart, a sadness filled his eyes.

His trial, by a "foreign" court, was held at Westminster Hall

He would not bow down to England's crown nor to their cabal

And the pre-determined verdict claimed that a "traitor's" death he'd face

And at Smithfield's Haberdasher's Hall, the gallows took their place.

Chained naked to a wooden frame, he was dragged o'er cobbled stones

Pelted by what came to hand as their King took up his throne

They laid his brutal body bare, ravaged by their fun-filled day

 And now he'd face his cruel death, not another word he'd say.

Hanged then dropped whilst still alive, the rope jerked his body tight

Then with joy they cut his manhood and burned them within his sight

His stomach slit then disembowelled, his entrails shown to the crowd

Then burned upon the brazier as their royalty had avowed.

The hangman held his knife aloft then opened up his chest,

And pulled out his warm, beating heart, a skill the hangman must possess

Then cut off his head and held it high for all the crowd to see

Then quartered up his body parts, all done by Royal decree.

His limbs were sent to Newcastle, to Berwick, Stirling, Perth,

The sentence for a Scottish knight for "their" treason on this earth

His head was spiked on Tower Bridge to embarrass Scotland's son

And to put the fear of Christ in Scots but that fear was all undone.

A barbaric death in barbaric times but it was a death held back for Scots

This butchery was the devil's work, another evil Royal plot

But tales of William Wallace spread and a martyr he became

And far beyond this island's realms Freedom claimed the Wallace name.

When a man stands up for his beliefs and stands up for what is right

No power can match the human faith, not even Royal might

Wallace lives in us today, in the heart of every Scot

But his Freedom is a right for all and not what we're being taught.

Different Streets.   5.8.17.

Brother, sister, don't you cross the line,

Stay home and close your doors

And keep your words within your minds

We don't need them anymore,

If you're after self-indulgence

Don't dare show your face

The world's a stage for everyone

But each should know their place,

You think you wander corridors

Against the power, the elite

But you are just the same as them,

Just born on a different street.

Distant Drums.   19.8.17

As they clatter through the silence

Of a Glasgow afternoon

The rain is thick and heavy

Just another Scots' monsoon

Drab and grey like yesterday

And yet, it's different today

I can't see them but I can hear

Their drums of bigotry.

The rolls of orange coloured tunes

Are disrupted by the snare

And as the rain pings off their holy hall

Their flutes join in the air

God knows what tune they're playing

I'd rather listen to the rain

With rain there is no bigotry,

With rain there is no pain.

Where the Silent Cry.   7.9.17.

The hidden corners of darkened nights

Are where the silent cry

We know they sleep in alleyways

But we'd rather pass them by

No-one wanders down their way

To face the truth we fear

No-one wants to feel their pain

Hypocrisy's so sincere.

We think of them, a little,

Cold, tired, hungry, wet

Some may be even close to death

And that's as good as it might get,

We think we know how they must feel

But in reality, we don't,

Rejection is so hard to take,

We'd love to help but won't.

We block them from society

We say, they don't belong to us

So, why do we feel so guilty

And why make all this fuss?

Scottish Dawn.   16.9.17

Who are these cretins? Does anyone know?

Where did they come from? Where did they go?

They weren't here yesterday yet hit the front page

Then appeared on our screens with their bile and rage.

With their prominence reached in the blink of an eye

I look to Westminster and begin to ask why,

I look to their puppets, the condemned BBC

And it seems there are many who are thinking like me.

So where did they come from and where did they go?

Did they come from Westminster, our reliable foe?

The Broken BBC.   20.9.17.

As you lay those sad, pathetic seeds

In some inferior brain

Remember those who will not feed

But scorn your bloodied reign

And as you scoff those who reject your views

It is you who bears that cost

For in turn we have rejected you

How many licences have you lost?

You say you'll do your utmost here

To clear your biased name

But you're doing absolutely nothing

You just carry on your shame

And negate our positivity

Filling more and more with rage

But until you feel your pockets bare

You'll just read that same old page.

You're so conceited you cannot see

The hate that's aimed at you

Instead, your smug and pompous staff

Ignore those points of view

From us, your owners, or at least,

Those who still pay your fee,

We know you're political puppets

And your talk is never free

You don't need much encouragement

To put this country down

You actually revel in this task,

You're a circus ruled by clowns.

You Can Call Me Prof.

Hello, I am Adam Tomkins, a typical Tory Toff

I get called all sorts of names but you can call me Prof.

I'm a tosser of the Enth Degree and a Unionist at heart

And I will rip, with all my might, your Scotland wide apart!

I'm the prick who shouts and bawls, I'm your Tory farce

I will always stand firm against you with Murdo up my arse.

Tory Fascists.   13.10.17.

As you banquet in Europe with your enemy hosts

Does your brain even function, let alone be engrossed?

You stand, looking stupid and the world ridicules

This lost greatness of Britain and a government of fools.

You can't answer questions, you've got nothing to say

You've lost all respect but you won't walk away,

Your Victorian values and your decadent ways

Belong in an Empire that has long since decayed.

You hang onto coat-tails and your posh dialogue

All buffed up and polished like Jacob Rees-Mogg

Where did you find him, what planet's he on?

He's The Tory who welcomes the Fascists' new dawn.

As this magnificence crumbles, what will remain?

You are nearing extinction with your infertile brain

It's paralysed, rotten, as you know only too well

May your god ride beside you as you charge into Hell!

Tory DUP.   **13.10.17.**

You sat down and discussed with a mob full of hate,

The ones who you tell us will make your Britain Great

You're a whore to the system and don't care who you bed,

To you, power is all, and it's gone to your head.

That bright orange bigoted sash that you wear

The one you all bow to but pretend it's not there,

Well look at you now, swathed in Orangemen's glee

And the party that wears it, is Arlene's DUP.

Is peace in the Provinces now out of your hands,

And how can you be neutral when you bow to demands?

You're inept with no power as you now share your calls

You're bent over a barrel, and they've got your balls.

Christianity According to Theresa May.

She falters to worship and feigns a wry smile,

Expecting her god to make her time worthwhile:

I bow down to no-one and do as I please

You bow to me, you get on your knees

For if I cleanse your earth showing meagre restraint

Then you will pardon my killings and make me a saint!

Ross Thomson, Proud Tory.   3.12.17.

Just hold a gun up to their heads, that is more humane

Than standing in a Tesco store for your own political gain,

Don't you feel embarrassed, don't you feel ashamed?

Look at your constituents with their anger inflamed!

You helped make this world a cruel, bitter place

A lying Tory hypocrite, just another waste of space,

You're asking ordinary people, people so unlike yourself

To feed the poorest you condemn, you don't buy lives on shelves!

And you stand there like a shining knight, collecting in your suit

An opportunist seeking fame in your Tory photoshoot,

Don't take the Scottish public to be the fools you think they are

When new elections come around, we'll roast your Tory arse.

You stir hatred in your public yet want to walk away immune

But you can't adorn exemption when it's you who caused the ruin,

There is bitterness, not sympathy, towards you and it's deserved

For on your own constituents, a death warrant's what you served.

You, installed the foodbanks! You, took away their pride,

The basic right to live a life, you, have them, denied.

You're not rationale in your thinking, you're a disturbed pathetic man

There is no grace in poverty which you progress throughout this land.

Strangled by Your Flag.   **5.12.17.**

Dear Conservatives and Unionists, you have done it once

Again

You walk on stilts, onto a stage, trying to look quite sane

And you almost get away with it, but then, the killer blow

is dealt

Those bigots from The DUP got you well and truly TELT!

That Brexit ship is now ablaze and you're being dragged
across its deck
And it's The DUP who's dragging you with a Union flag
'round your neck
The noose is tightened thick and fast but no-one hears
your screams
Your marriage made in heaven is now one hellish dream!
The Union flag you hold so dear is in tatters, torn and
Frayed
They held you up for ransom with that ransom duly paid
How do you feel this morning, there's been no sight or
Sound
And your strong and stable government are nowhere to be
found!

Big Dick.   11.12.17.

Has there ever been more incompetence
Than what we're witnessing today?
It's a political epidemic

And Richard Leonard leads the way,

He's the one they call Messiah

But we know him as Dick

Just another Labour Unionist

Just another useless prick.

Every session's an embarrassment

Where he just gets ripped apart

With no belief in what he says

And no belief within his heart.

Who writes these scripts for him to fail

And are they checked before the show,

What's devolved and what's reserved,

It's these basics they don't know!

It's like watching kids at primary school

But it's too painful for a laugh

It is pitiful to watch this clown

As he drowns himself with gaffes.

Is this all that Labour has,

Is he really Scotland's best?

Look around at what talent's left

And they're not exactly blessed!

Their Silent Plea.   11.12.17.

The ice is here and the freezing nights
Bring sleeping bags with no-one in sight
They're huddled up and out of view
And wishing, now, that they were you.

What you see is not really there,

We're living out a lie

But the unkind world we live in

Is as real as you or I,

We don't see children on the street

Or the doorway girl at night

To some they're just obstructions

And our city streets, they blight.

We treat them worse than animals

Because they're destitute and poor

So they're buffeted from street to street

And then from door to door,

Once dignified we've broken them

Their silence is their plea,

Don't think these people don't exist

Because you refuse to see.

It's The Poorest Who Must Die!   12.12.17.

Your halcyon days are over, your destiny's been sealed

Your cruel reign is almost done with your frailties all revealed,

Corruption stands beside you, he is always by your side

Yet another whose corruption is one we can't abide.

This man and wife together would bring four nations to its knees

Putting health beyond the poor and inflicting forced disease

You've annihilated thousands through the gold you hold so dear

Your Christian values bought you, your very own Trail of Fears!

Your existence is not humble and never was it sweet

On you, religion's wasted, you only captured its deceit

Maybe your god is on your side but a devil has your back

You do not know compassion as you prepare your next attack.

And it's always the poor who suffer, always those who need the most

But you insist upon their suffering, quietly killing, like a ghost,

You prepare your media for the news then slide out some new bill

Another one to hurt the poor, you don't care who you kill!

For they are of no consequence, they are expendable at best

And at least you can sleep at night, knowing there'll be no inquest!

Your compelling passion for a deity was your greatest ever lie

But you'll always be remembered for, "It's the poorest who must die!"

David Davis. 12.12.17.

(About a punch-drunk illiterate liar).

An agreement that they all stood by, they're now abandoning with ease

We don't need to acknowledge it! Now that's a government of sleaze

While their joyous media applaud and cheer from the ramparts of their tower,

Their unwillingness to admit it's false, leaves their usual sordid glower

Fixed on disruptive peasants, who they cast aside at will

Whilst knowing their complicity has yet to reach that overkill.

This punch-drunk illiterate liar, is the guy they put in charge

He's The Tories' Tommy Cooper, their comedian at large

A hundred years have almost passed, yet Westminster struggles on

This government's "deal" on Brexit is now being challenged by its own

They're now under the world's microscope and mistrust is what they see

Kick back Scotland, wildly, and set your country free!

This is Power! 12.12.17.

You struggle with the acceptance that Southern Ireland's free

You still cling to an ancient past and your barbaric history,

Eire owes you nothing except a mutual respect

But even that's a massive struggle and one, some still reject.

They're now telling past suppressors what they can and cannot do

Because the British Brexit Eejits have not a single clue

And while the rabid Bulldog bares its teeth and stares Karma in the face,

It stares upon the upstart's flag yet still feels no disgrace.

It's irked by its incessant failure to accept they might be wrong

And, of course, that Eire, proudly, is singing her own song

But Eire's not being difficult, it's only playing by EU rules

Rules that seem so alien to the UK's Brexit fools!

The Empire never will strike back, it is finished, it is done

But in their manic arrogance, these idiots think they've won

And when our referendum comes around, and one day soon it will,

We'll reflect upon the Irish and feel the power of that thrill.

It's an independent country with powers not extreme

I only hope that Scotland next time has the conviction of her dreams.

Branson.   14.12.17.

This parasitic billionaire's no virgin at this game

For life to him is nothing if he can't have wealth and fame

Forget about the plastic smile, he's starring in his show,

Barking out his orders and drinking his Bordeaux

While laughing down at all of us, he sues the NHS

This guy's no bloody angel, he's a man that is possessed

But he can't allow his audience to catch him off his guard

Especially when he's hitting them and hitting them bloody hard.

He's amassed a fortune and it's us who're made to pay

This nice old smiling Virgin man, milks us every day,

He's an army of auditors and lawyers standing by his side

Ensuring every note is crisp and all is legal, bona fide

And then he can rub his grimy hands and give himself a cheer

Before heading to his Paradise where the bankers close their ears!

Murdo Fraser.
(The unthankful Murdo blocked me after I wrote this for him).

We're poles apart in everything

But I thought we could be friends

Another Tory liar in Scotland

So I rebuked him 'til the end.

His words degrade my country

Which he lavishes with intent

My words were only aimed at him,

Every, triggered, sentiment!

There was no need to embarrass him

He does that on his own

I was the only friend he ever had

And now he's all alone.

I took to Twitter, late last night

And was visibly shaken, shocked

For those honest words I aimed at him

Led me to being blocked.

A degenerate had blocked me!

He didn't even know my name!

To him I'm just The Indy Poet,

And sees me Scotland's shame!

A man who entered competitions

But had yet to win just one

A man who'd never been elected

Yet a List vote meant he'd won!

Just a self-confessed egoist

Probably the best there's ever been

Who held his Royal Standard proudly

By the portrait of his queen

A Unionist in every sense

But couldn't tell the truth from lies

He had hatred, badly hidden,

Which helped my last goodbyes.

He was just like Ferris Bueller

Dogging days off school

But that led to one at Holyrood

Make him look a bloody fool.

He's on Twitter when he's working

This Tory Tweeting god

But I won't report old Murdo

That would just add to Tory Fraud

I know you want to make an impact

So proudly spout your point of view,

I know you want to be in Westminster

But who would really vote for you?

For now I'll say goodbye my friend

You're one of a special kind

A typical anti-Scottish Tory

And right out of your tiny, little mind.

The Frightened Rabbit. 16.12.17.

Stuck in the headlights, like an animal trapped

He trembles and freezes as though he's been zapped,

This frightened rabbit's motionless but then slowly starts to speak

And stumbles to that nervous state we witness every week.

Flailing arms are trying to say the words he can't get out

He steps his voice increasingly, but the truth remains a doubt

His shaking words are utterances but then he screams and bawls

And waves his flailing arms like some loony in a brawl

He shouts at those he dares to blame from his immoral ground

And bemuses all who hear him, with his incoherent sounds.

His mildness turns to anger, his face now, shades of red

His contorted body jerks and twists as though he's poison fed

He can bask, for now, in glory as he knows he's near his end

But in our fight for Independence, he's been our Independent friend!

Poor old Richard Leonard, you were doomed right from the start

Frightened rabbits never win, they lack conviction and a heart!

Annie Wells MSP.   18.12.17.

She worked in Marks and Spencer, a manageress of note

And the working class of Glasgow gave this woman votes

But now she ridicules them and sees them as no good

For she plays the high and mighty now she's in Holyrood.

The Complicit BBC.   18.12.17.

They don't do Bias voluntarily, that's a perk, the poor man's curse

Monies paid to The Tory cause, in an already swollen purse

It's a Tory run establishment with every boss decked out in blue

53

Where Executives and subordinates, fight for their
precious few.

Not A Burden.   **20.12.17.**

Where did yer village go

Ah thought ye'd like tae know

It wis taken while they cut oot yer tongue

Noo there's naeb'dy left to grow

The seeds o' hate they sewed

Urr ye lookin' fur a song that's needin' sung?

Freedom's no' the burden

They wid huv us a' believe

Where were a' their kind words when

They left us a' tae grieve?

Oor forebears died fur freedom

They thought it worth the fight

Now's the time to claim back

What was always Scotland's right.

They took away yer plaid

An' its wearing they forbade

Then bundled ye tae some shore faraway

The leavin' cut their hearts

As their lives were ripped apart

Still some don't hear the message they convey.

Chorus.

The crofts now lie around

Sae sparsely on the ground

Crumblin' tae the earth that lies below

And the legacy they've shared

Is that their masters didnae care,

Keep closer still the ones you do not know.

Chorus.

The Empty Banks of The Clyde.   **28.12.17.**

There's a peacefulness, a silence

You've that emptiness you craved

How different from the past I knew

And all this river gave

I look down the flowing river

Now so tranquil and serene

It's a lonely Clyde that passes by

With nothing in between

Our industries were taken

When they should have been enshrined

Is now a cultured desolation,

Desolation by design.

The Green Ink Gang.   **Hogmanay 2017.**

They crawl inside their tiny minds

And close their corporate door

Where they plot and plan their letters

Like unfavourable little whores

Their choice of topic? Hatred!

And each one a Tory ned

Who say they fight for Scotland

While they really want her dead!

Each are sworn to secrecy

Whose names can't be revealed,

Their identity, for the Union's sake

Must always be concealed.

They're The Union's Secret Service

Funded by their rich regime

And write, not as individuals,

But as a hateful right-wing team.

Keyboards pound out day and night

As they fire off their posts

And complicit in this utter sham

Are their genial Union hosts,

Letters by the thousands

Are sent daily to our rancid press

All signed off by these conspirators

With the hand of bitterness.

But as always there's a failing one

Who breaks cowardly, sordid rules

As the names of all were printed out

Showing the world this ship of fools.

Names already known to us

Sprung onto our screens

The Green Ink Gang they call themselves

But they're anything but Green.

How will their donors now react

As their names are known too?

The Green Ink Gang now writhe and squirm

In their flag red, white and blue.

My River.   1.1.18.

You surge along with such a force,

You burst your bonnie banks

Then tranquil as a summer breeze

You bless our hearts with thanks,

You have no destination

Your journey has no end

You're always moving, never stop,

Not even for a friend.

Twisting, turning, rolling on,

Your strength it knows no bounds

Yet in graceful, melancholic mood

Your beauty still astounds.

You bask then tail off in the night

Like a silken silver band,

A ribbon wafting easily

Lighting up our midnight land

But you rise in all your glory

In the early morning mist

When your castles stand, salute you

And your trees bow for a kiss.

You're no more than a stream in parts

But in others, deep and wide

You're the lifeblood of our city

You are my River Clyde.

Culloden's Red Skies.   **5.1.18**

While some fought for religion others fought for a crown

Some gave up their sons for their own hallowed ground

But despised was the coward for his own selfish acts

And none felt for the father who signed this evil pact.

You forfeited sons for the sake of your land

Then signed their death warrants with your devious hand

As you sent one, a rebel, for the Jacobite cause

To oppose his own brother, the one who gained your

applause.

As they faced each other with their father's steel swords

Which one would fall, the Laird's or the Lord's

He was willing to pay for a lifestyle so grand

With the death of a son by the other son's hand!

Some fought for their freedom, some fought for a crown

But here, they are both dead, on a blood sodden ground

Culloden's still crying at a war that was won

When brother fought brother and father killed son.

The sun sets on secrets but they're awakened at dawn

When sunlight unravels that his sons were but pawns

He betrayed his own sons for the sake of some land

And cut both them down with his cowardly hand.

He had no sense of honour or pride, dignity

There's no escape for the guilty, they can never be free

Sadly, many were like him and thousands still are

They gained land, blessed with fortune, that would heal all
their scars.

On the field of the killings the sky was turned red

Reflecting the blood of all sons lying dead,

Their ghosts look for loved ones with tears in their eyes

As their deaths are reflected in Culloden's red skies.

Your Castle on a Hill.

Ye perch yersels on Calton Hill

Or a hill by any name

And play yer fiddles tae the tune

Whilst ignoring a' the flames

Kings and Queens some think ye are

In yer castles in the sky

And do nothing as yer country burns,

As oor cultures fade an' die.

Ye watched the crofters sail away

And those who stayed lay dead

Burnt alive within their homes

Or when rafters crushed their heads.

Oor ancient tongue sae colourful

Was cut oot by the sword

And aye, we stood and watched the foe

That bastard Scottish Lord.

And like the sheep that roamed the land

Being fattened for the kill

We stand and watch those deaths again

From oor castle on a hill.

Like then oor tongues are silent

As though the past has been restored

Some will speak whilst others won't

They still fear their overlords.

The Warlords and You.   9.1.18.

In my lifetime I've witnessed many crimes, many wars

Most committed by policies, all endorsed by the Lords

Yet politicians are lauded for the deaths of our own

All abetted and aided by the queen on her throne.

We've a government unable to back what they propose

And a weak opposition who refuse to oppose

We have psychopaths ruling with incompetent flair

Who show by their killings, the extent of their care.

They bring back the old guard to kill off those who survived

They're a killing machine but YOUR vote lets them thrive

Try telling the near-dead you walk passed every day

Or the soldiers, discarded, who're now wasting away

You allow their dreams to manifest within their crippled minds

Without the realisation, you are the tie that binds

Yet I see no resistance, no fight, you feel no blame,

But the saddest thing's, these killings are, all blessed in
your bloody name!

The Cost of Free Speech.   **11.1.18.**

Speech is free with fortunes paid

By the richest in our midst

Telling us, the under-privileged,

Our opinions don't exist,

But our tongues will not be silenced

And we are meant to be impressed

By their divisive monologue

Which cannot be redressed.

We will never have their riches,

These dictators run the show

We are the minds suppressed by them

The ones who cannot know

But as they see the people rising

They don't like what they hear

The people now have wakened

And it's now them who live in fear.

Deserters.   **17.1.18.**

Westminster is our Alamo

Where the bravest cross the line

Hand-picked to fight for Scotland

Their names they proudly signed

Others said they'd stand beside us

And would be honoured, proud to serve

For once, we felt part honesty,

As we called on our reserves.

We have all the ammunition

But as we led this last attack

Our reservists are deserters

Who just shoot us in the back.

We may stumble through this battle

And together, win this war

But for those who won't stand with us

Just who are they fighting for?

The Chieftain.   **25.1.18.**

As you gaze upon your feast tonight

And recite our honoured bard

Be thoughtful of the words you use

And those you might discard

For thoughts of Independence

Flow through his every line

And only those who're blinded

Can't read his Independent mind.

As the Chieftain lays before you

And plaudits you endow,

Can't you feel the bitter tears

Pouring from his bow

For the cordial words you grant him

Not only hurt but bind

His hatred for a Union

Through his Independent mind.

Drink up and give an honest toast

To the brother of all men

For in our hearts we'll never feel

The likes of him again.

The Scottish Thirteen.

I'll tell you a story of The Scottish Thirteen

They're a renegade band who have never been seen

They fed you with fortunes, they fed you with lies

They asked for your cross and you truly obliged.

What they wouldn't do and what you couldn't be

You thought they were truly concerned

But they saw you were blind and got into your mind

Do you now think your lesson's been learned?

They used all their charm to bring you self-harm

And like fools, you drank to their health

If you believed what they said then you're sick in the head

It was all about them and their wealth.

We're the world's only nation where their education

Teaches us to hate our own land

And through repetition, they mould us, condition

'Til we bow and say, "we understand".

But some of us don't and more of us won't

With thousands more ready to rise

If you look deep down inside and get yourself back your pride

You'll see Independence is your greatest prize.

That House.   **28.1.18.**

The grey haired and blue rinse brigade

Lay idly on their thrones

With the exception of that honoured Scot,

Our Lady Michelle Mone.

She's seldom there, rarely votes

And is rightly criticised,

But this self-made queen of lingerie

Still loads her Tory gun with lies.

Aye, she may stay awake when there

Unlike those who need their sleep

Sleeping from their drunken lunch

While the rest of Britain weeps,

Red noses show they've too much port

Their tongues are spirits lined

With some words barely audible

Through their penchant for fine wines.

This Baroness of Mayfair,

Lest we forget, her OBE

Wants Scotland shackled to this Union

And never to be free

So who will speak for Scotland

Is there one we can award

The honour of our nation

In this parlour called The Lords?

We have an unelected House down there

With no Lords, SNP

They abhor all that I stand for

So who will speak for me?

Traitors In Our Land.

They threaten us with treason, we are traitors in our own
land

We're being treacherous in their cruel regime where the
blood is on *their* hands

We are pretentious little upstarts, seen as rebels with no
cause,

And want to sanctify and cleanse us by overturning all our
laws

But in our attempt to thwart their scavenging and revoking
all they crave

They continue with austerity, seeking more for early graves

We're their contemptuous tartaned natives whose hopes
upset their plans

Yet they fear our sheer audacity to empower our own land.

The Street Doesn't Care.   **2.2.18.**

They'll manipulate, use you and do all to abuse you

They're the cancer that runs through your veins

But they don't need to hide when the media's onside

They'll convince you they're feeling your pain.

They cut every service but you can't see this dis-service

While you believe every word that they say

And the next time you're ill, you might get a bill

I just hope your insurance can pay.

When you're thrown on the streets because of bills you can't meet

You paid up but it wasn't enough

Or you paid with your home and now, your city, you roam

You'll find out what it's like sleeping rough.

You look for a bench in, a city entrenched in

Neighbours who thought they had class

But the street doesn't care, you put yourself there

Now it's you who'll count those who walk passed!

The Band is Back.

Democracy is on the move marching to a tartan beat

With Saltires flying high once more on every Scottish street

Hearts are reignited and they're dancing to a tune

For the pipes and drums are playing: "We'll Be
Independent Soon".

They'll be hanging out their tenements to watch the great
parade

Some of you will walk down streets where, as children, you
once played,

If you know an undecided, bring them in, give them a hand

For we're all on the same journey to our Independent land.

You'll get the wave, the nod, the wink, the smiles from
passers-by

You'll get the car horns beeping and drivers shouting Aye!

Some shoppers will give you dirty looks; some will even
think they're grand,

They'll free money from their wallets while you march to
free your land.

I hear you chant, I see you laugh, I've been there and it's
fun

And the road that you now travel is for your daughters and
your sons

So grab your friends and neighbours, walk together side by
side

Make them feel Independent and let them share your
pride.

It's a spectacle of colour where you get to meet new friends,

And I'm talking from experience, those friendships never end

They're always there beside you, always there to lend a hand

They're The Independence Movement and they just want back their land.

Bring those who fear a government that will send them from our shores

Call all our EU citizens let them know we've open doors

And that immigrants are welcome to march with us today,

Together we'll go forward to our Independence Day.

I Am Not British. 1.2.18.

We are British through enforcement

And that's a word that's much maligned

But the atrocities that go with it

Can never enter feeble minds.

You can hide behind your finery

Or underneath your Butcher's rag

But your history you'll never know

For your Lawlords keep you gagged.

Your ignorance is paramount

To the ones you idolise, adore

And as long as there are sheep like you

We will live in those days of yore.

What are these British values

That you pronounce with so much pride?

It's just your modern stance on bigotry

From a past you try to hide!

You proudly fly the British Union flag

Whilst you burn your country's own

Then, with fervour, sing its anthem

Whilst Scotland's, you disown!

You tell me Britain is a nation

But a nation it is not

Scotland is my country

And I will always be a Scot.

Vultures. 3.2.18.

While Westminster pores o'er ill-gotten gains

Scots look upon their last remains

Will you stand with me this Yes Campaign

And break these stately chains?

It is not on England I protest

It is Westminster that I detest

For far too long we've been suppressed

Let Scotland now progress.

They're eroding Scotland day on day

With cunning stealth they eat away

Consuming all who're in their way

They're the vultures, we're the prey.

The Tank. 1.3.18.

For many years I've listened to,

And listened without fear,

The Tank Commander's utterances

And seen smiles through her tears

But with gallantry she charges on

Like a rebel with a cause

But unarmed with the brain she needs

To escape our FM's claws.

How inept she is as leader,

How absurd her questions asked

And how easy it is, for our FM,

To bring The Tory's Tank to task!

Hands Off Our Parliament.   24.3.18.

(My sincere thanks to Cliff Serbie, Dave Llewelyn and everyone who helped make this a phenomenal day).

As I alit at Waverley, my expectancy was high

But my heart sank in expectancy as the crowds just passed me by

No Saltires draped 'round shoulders, the signs were not too good

And so, despondently, I took the path, that led to Holyrood.

A dozen folk before me with the same garnered behind

Was this all that Scotland offered, was our country so maligned?

I know it was a working day but sadness filled my heart

This indifference to a power grab was tearing me apart.

But then I came upon its grounds, awash with happy hordes

They were packed into the entrance, holding placards, hoisting boards,

My heart jumped at this revelry and pumped with great relief

That Scotland once again, when asked, had shown her true belief.

Thousands stood and swirled around, mingling with their friends

And all past negativity seemed to vanish without end,

On and on they poured in droves and laughter filled these grounds

From every corner of these lands where friendship knows no bounds.

A Chinese television crew interviewed, filmed in full view

But that famous British media just seemed to pass on through

While our speakers spoke and singers sang, some took time out to dance

And our supposed Scottish media, never threw a second glance.

We circled Scotland's parliament, our hands joined together by pride

A task we could have undergone with four deep side by side

Then we heard our Bikers thunderous roar as they circled round the green

But the noise, the cheers, the running crowds was almost now routine.

They stood in awe, excited, as cameras snapped with glee

Old and young climbed steps to view, and that included me,

The Bikers heightened up that buzz and they circled round the track

And screamed out loud to everyone; Yes, Now! The Band is back!

Exhilarations and a dignity replaced our nation's deep despair

And quashed the threat of London's house, because for them, we do not care

We've a national pride they can't consume, they'll never understand or know

And our answer to this unhinged mob, is their favourite word, that's No!

Bridges for Indy.   25.3.18.

(I was asked to write a wee tune for BfI by Mike Fenwick and this was the result).

Have you bridges beside you that look empty and bare

Could you not decorate them with some good Scottish fayre

Should the beauty of Scotland not be hanging there

Well, stand with your Saltires and feel all that it bears.

We're Bridges for Indy whose flags you see fly

We are the silence, you see passing by

We're the Cross of St Andrew's that lights up your sky

So if you see us above you, just toot! and shout Aye!

We fly not these favouring, race, colour, creed

Nor by sexual alignment or need for your greed

We're patriotic, we're people who were borne from a seed

Our aim's Independence and we need you to succeed.

When obstacles block us, our friendship extends

For it's for the love of our country that we must defend

But for the love of a country we can't always depend

There are those who would rather be ruled by our friends.

Our Yes Movement's growing with a quickening pace

Where we all are leaders and seek only Scotland's embrace

So, join us this weekend, let the wind feel your face

Let your own Independence have its own rightful place.

Every motorway must see our Saltires flown

Every bridge in this country we must make our own

There are many injustices we must now atone

And this Union's the first that we'll see overthrown.

Sleepy Hollow.   9.4.18.

It's the Mother of all Parliaments

Where the fucked-up congregate,

A medieval sleepy-hollow

Where they tire of debate,

Eyes closed own in restful mode

Their minds and bodies limp

Dreaming of expenses

While the poorest of us scrimp.

This Temple of the afflicted

Is where death enacts its laws,

An asylum of corruption,

Where humans send their flaws.

Death is their agenda

And it's you they're out to get

You are their expendables

And yet you hold them in your debt,

They fed you their illusion

As they led you to your death

Then laughed loudly in their corridors

As you breathed your dying breath.

Children of War.   **22.4.18.**

As you send your children out to war

There's a tear in either eye

You prepared them for a life ahead

But didn't tell them how to die,

You watch them slowly walk away

Remembering all they ever were

And in that moment, drifting,

They are no longer there.

Flowing tears replace lost words

There is no comfort here

But those memories of mind and heart

Will always keep them near

But that's all you'll have, just memories,

As fear becomes part of your day

But their life is no longer just their own

And dreams, are all washed away.

They're now the establishment's servant

Where the peacemaker learns his new skill,

They're not told the truth of their carnage

They're just given a licence to kill.

NO to YES.

There's mair tae us than meets the eye

An' mair tae us than rallies

Aye, we'll protest a' that's wrang

Then blether ower swallies

But why we March, ye'll never know,

Ye jist take a wild guess

But if you could see past a' their lies,

Then you too wid be YES.

Admiring Chains.   23.4.18.

You were always a child of this country

And her child you will always remain

But some don't know they are prisoners

They're too busy admiring their chains.

We're all aliens trapped in their Union

Where your freedom has no right of talk

You are clapped in their irons of justice

With your head clamped down on their block.

Don't you know of the story that binds you

It's their prison and they hold the key

They gave you the shackles you're wearing

And yet you think you are free!

Why do you bow to the knowledge of strangers

And accept all that you are told

When you question their lies and their arrogance

You'll see you are being controlled.

They have starved us of progress and fortune,

Saying we are too weak on our own

Now's the time to prove to all Scotland

We'll be fine going it alone.

Dun Phris.

Will ye take me sae kindly,

Ma heart an' ma' soul,

Will ye walk wi' me gently,

Shall we take a wee stroll

Right doon tae the borders

Tae march on Dumfries

Dear Fluffy awaits us

Wi' his new private police.

I hear that he bides in

A quaint little toon

An' ah hear it'll be hoachin'

Oan the second o' June

An' ah hope the Doonhammers

Like the rest o' us Scots

Are fed up wi' the ramblins

O' their most infamous Scot.

It's another wee party

We jist love days away

An' if Fluffy's no' up f'rit

Can he get Theresa May?

Donald Netanyahu.   9.5.18.

He has no sense of justice, of loyalty,

He's Trump and he's King

But as long as he's "telling the truth"

You won't do a thing

Why do you stand back and applaud

Israel's nuclear regime?

Why do you allow this,

Is this Your American Dream?

Netanyahu's your gaffer

But America, you're too blind to see

And with Congress pulling the strings

Your puppet's been freed

The orange man's psyche is bought

He's no words of his own

And he's telling you right to your face

It's **YOU** he will disown!

Al-Qaeda, White Helmets and Isis

They're all one and the same

Funded by you and Israelis

In their great killing game

Don't tell me of necessary wars

They don't now exist

They'll have you hate colour and creed

And then you'll enlist!

You protest on the streets with your kids

To banish all guns

Yet vote for these massacres abroad

And cheer like it's fun

We are ruled by some mad men and women

And you, you made yourselves whores

For your god's sake for once use your brain

Tell them this land is yours!

Iran has great wealth and you've not,

That! is the whole of your clue

And the UK is fully compliant

With the Israeli's view,

Iran isn't starting a war

After centuries of peace,

Look to your military then weep

When you count your deceased!

Your Judgement.   10.5.18.

You came out loaded with your gun

And shot me down, was that for fun?

And left me in a pool of blood just lying

Your god came down absolved your sins

And healed your darkened soul within

Then winked at me when he saw me dying.

Your god's a fool and so are you

You don't know if he's catholic, Jew

But all of you are killing one another

Muslim, Hindu, white or black

Each one will stab you in the back

Don't you know you're killing your own brother?

Your Holy Bible makes no sense

Its stars are lawyers in defence

Each claiming some indifference they think good

It's starred in every war that's been

And many deaths found in between

And still you tell me, I misunderstood!

I hoped one day we'd all be friends,

It's too late now to make amends

But I hope our children never fight each other

I'm lying here, tears in my eyes

You never even said goodbye

You didn't even know I was your brother.

Who is the persecutor here

The one with hope, the one with fear?

Judgement's with the one you represent

That's you my friend if you don't know

When life is done, you close the show

And take with you, the love, that they resent!

Failing Palestine and Humanity.   **11.5.18.**

(My response to Jackson Carlaw who wants to build Bridges with Israel).

You want us to build Bridges while you reject ours

You scan our words and all we say, with your faces always soured

And the Bridges you want us to build are with a killing state

Controlled by Netanyahu from a position filled with hate.

You want us to enhance their wealth and be welcomed by their love

I wish there really was a god and that he'd strike you from above

You see, I'd rather go to Palestine to relax and have a ball

Not to dodge Israeli bullets or be ushered through great concrete walls.

I want to breathe the local culture, to hear laughter, children play,

I don't want to turn a corner and see them blown away

I want to visit local restaurants and see families enjoy meals

Not half a fucking family because of Tories and their deals!

And you've the cheek to ask me to enhance your wealthy chums

Tell me, is it any wonder, you're known as Tory Scum?

I am not anti-Semitic, I am just a normal man

A man, the same the world over, who wants peace in every land,

A man who wants men like you, who fund that killing state

To stand in front of Palestinians and explain to them their fate.

Tell them why their fathers died, their mothers, sisters, sons,

Tell them that you aided The Israelis and their guns

Tell them everything you know, that you're a part of that regime

Tell them that you never flinch when you're the children scream!

Tell them that you're sorry, that their daughters have been jailed

And lastly say you're sorry, it was humanity, you failed!

The Last Line!   15.5.18.

Mundell and his cronies have ignored us once more,

Doing again as they please

It's a Union of Equals, this cretin demands

Then tells Scotland, get back on your knees!

He's May's human shield, her last line of defence

A last line that couldn't be worse

He's too busy eating the scraps of his beard,

Fine dining must always come first!

But you'd better remind him of what you request

His attention span's not what it was

But he'll still claim expenses, whilst bringing his own,

With greed the most probable cause!

Scottish Chancers.   16.5.18.
(A Rip-off of The Killers' song, karaoke anyone)?

Say goodbye to Independence

You will hear of it no more

Say goodbye to Caledonia

And remain Westminster's whores

And when you're all complaining,

Think of why you voted No!

We'll be there,

Reminding you,

We told you so!

Chorus.

Are you Scottish

Or just a Chancer

Our land will go

Because of you

And as you scratch your head

Looking for the answers,

Are you Scottish

Or just a Chancer?

Say goodbye to foreign romance

And your European friends

Because England's made arrangements

For all those loves to end

Don't indulge yourself in thinking

It's not good for the soul

For they've agreed

It's Scotland's right

To be controlled.

Chorus.

I know you're feeling nervous

You've surrendered your old ways

But if they say you'll be deported

We will fight for you to stay

Scotland stands beside you

While their hatred they instil,

They don't care

They never have

They never will.

Chorus.

On Our Day of Independence

When this Union is dissolved

We can all be brothers, sisters

And tell The Tories we've evolved

They're finished here in Scotland

They are out there all alone

I hope the family

That they love

Will claim their own.

Chorus.

The Stolen Streets.   **18.5.18.**

(The Homeless in Windsor dragged away because of a royal wedding).

Upon this street for many years

I have made and known my bed

And now, upon this eighteenth day,

I return to lay my head.

Here, I met a cloak-ed gentleman

As I made down for the night,

I thought of him as well-to-do,

Rather elegant by sight,

I made myself acquainted

And he acknowledged my request

With a smile I'd never seen before

Which unhinged my thoughts of rest!

He murmured low with increased tone

And a pitch, I felt, obscene

Till with fervour, crushed rebellious Scots,

All in favour of his queen.

I eased an open eye to him,

Then allowed it wander round

And saw his gabble revel royally

Dancing round a plastic crown.

Most were gentry from abroad

Beyond that great and civil wall

I believe from Watford going north

Where the heathen makes the call,

Old dears dressed like painted dolls

Clothed in hideously made suits

Strange bedfellows I must insist

They all sleep wearing boots.

Of Course! This is a charitable ball,

Gad, what splendidness I thought!

But there was something strange and rather odd

That rendered this, as not!

These gawdy suits, so bright and loud

Why had they all come here?

They were neither fiend nor friendly

But instilled in me a fear!

Where were my friends, my allies?

I now felt quite estranged!

These were not my gallant knights

But a people quite deranged!

I heard them in colloquial voice

Speak and sing to dolls

Struth! I thought unto myself

Their brains need overhauled!

They cuddled them and held them high

Then kissed them on the cheeks

Gadzooks! I cried to Windsor's men

Your streets are full of freaks!

Hush now sir, a calming voice,

Now whispered in my ear;

Confound you Sir, my strict reply,

Are my words not true and clear?

I'd bullwhip every one of them

By god, I'd strike them down

But he just smiled, left me to my own,

In my beloved Windsor town.

I felt unsafe in this melee

And forsook my thought of rest

Then heard my gallant knights were moved,

To a place their queen thought best,

A great assumption on my part

But none had intervened

All this while Windsor's outlanders

Still sang about their queen.

Red eyed, wearied wanderers

With strange concocted face

Had shamefully, in ill-fitting cloth,

Had, my gallant knights, replaced.

These ladies, painted marionettes,

Spoke with frog-like voice

Or perhaps the croak of wisdom

Had aged their sultry noise

And what of all their lurching men

With leering laughing eyes

What devil lies beneath thon look

What weirdness is disguised?

Alas! I gazed upon my street

My home for many years

Now taken by half-witted fools

For their circumstantial cheers.

For these, my gallant knights have gone

For these, my friends were spurned

But tomorrow when the dusk's begun

My bedmates will return

And we will take our corner

And prepare our fellow man

To share in all we have to give

In England's, green and pleasant land.

Sound, Liverpool.   18.5.18.
(Liverpool's Alternative Royal Celebrations).

There are creeps and weirdos with their friends

Camped out for fucking days on end

To catch a glimpse of two people getting wed

For you, Windsor's the place to be,

Cry your tears of joy on bended knee

But to me, you lot are off your fucking head!

In Liverpool they're showing the way

An alternative to The Royalist's Day

With "Fuck The Royals" staged to raise some funds

So get down to "Sound" and meet 'n' greet

And help those who can't afford to eat,

This is more than just The Scousers having fun.

Without canapes and caviar

They'll be jumping in that wee Scouse bar

Making sure that all locals there are fed

They don't need stupid hats or silly suits,

They're free thinking guys who know their roots

They are feeding those who just might end up dead!

Credit where credit's due

There are millions here saluting you

You're testament to all who really care

You've proved humanity exists

Something Royals just dismiss

May your locals go to bed with more than prayers.

Arse.   19.5.18.

(Douglas Ross, linesman extraordinaire on his extraordinary fall).

A ba' rolls tae the linesman

As he's prancin' doon the line

An' like some weird demented fairy

He springs intae pantomime

Ring o' ring o' roses

He clatters tae the grun

An' fifty thousand fitba' fans

A' cheered in Hampden's sun.

Has this guy ever kicked a ba'

He cannae keep his feet

Looks like the only balance this guy knows

Is on expenses sheets.

The Labour Ludge o' Falkirk.　　20.5.18.

When ye sleep wi' Tories an' fund the ludge,

Is it wrang that we complain

Or wid ye rather we ignored ye

An' yer increasing public pain?

Keep yer twisted bigotry

Fae the mooths of a' oor weans

An' keep yer rabble tae yersels

Wrapped in yer racist chains.

Don't play the high an' mighty

Playin' up tae former glories

Remember that yer colour

Is the shade of a' red Tories!

And Still Waiting.   20.5.18.

Just how equal is this Union

When we are tied to London's truss?

I asked the good and wise in Government

What do they do for us?

To my question I sought answers,

Clear, honest and precise

And looked forward to a thought-out plan,

Well-presented and concise,

One so beneficial to the Scots,

They would challenge sceptic minds

But alas, there are no answers,

And accept you're disinclined.

I seek no joyous self-appraisal

But your absence of replies,

Only builds our Independence cause

And this Union's quick demise.

Act One.   22.5.18.

As thespians one, nay, thespians all

They stepped out from the dark,

Their irony hung heavy,

Deep and coarse and stark,

Was this a betrayal of the love

That Cesar's friends had spurned

Or one more empire ending

As Nero watched his burn?

Power given then removed

By the senates of that day

Will lead to their destruction

As the words of might betray.

Their hollow words amused us

And we felt their trembling fear

They felt the knives of justice

Drawing ever near.

They fight with all their false beliefs

But know their end is nigh

And severed heads will duly roll

And belong to them, not I.

One Eye on The Time.   **22.5.18.**

Like a drug they're addicted to their chosen profession

And made our Independence their foremost obsession

Their prodigal son came hurtling back and stood on his new crate

While Darling stood in ermine in a line-up full of hate.

That bastard's in The House of Lords while Murphy works for Blair

And it doesn't matter where Ruth is, so long's a mic is there

Putting on her party act and spouting yet more lies

Then jokes with Arlene Fraser whom she clearly must despise!

Labour and The Tories are the same with different names

Different colours, personnel, playing their Scottish national game,

Down in London failing us with one eye on the time

For they know our clock is ticking down, with Independence chimes!

Their Great Profiteers.   24.5.18.

By refusing to bend to that place we despise

We're the nuisance, a folly, a mistake in their eyes

But we are not the coincidence they would have us assume

And we are not here for them, to corrupt and consume.

Their greatest concoction is that they're the aggrieved

And that we are the haters, the poor, under-achieved,

We must fight back with a voice that is heard and is feared

And forever banish those lies of the great profiteers.

They're the socially inept, more Scots who've been bought,

They can't change their spots and be someone they're not

We've heard all they've offered, every line they have
penned

All scripted, delivered and signed off, Scotland's friend

But we're now fighting for something that money can't buy

We are fighting for Scotland, and if we don't, she will die.

Arlene Foster, DUP.   1.6.18.

They're marching through Fife

And think we are impressed

With a real guest of honour

But she's no honourable guest

She'll lead from the front

In The Boyne Orange Walk

Then this shit for brains racist

Will deliver her talk,

She'll discharge her brain

With her abnormal thoughts

Bringing Unionist bigotry

Down on like-minded Scots.

As Northern Ireland's First Minister

Her Assembly collapsed

And since the battle they praise

Three hundred years have elapsed!

They live in the past

With blood up to their knees

Scotland's trying to move forward

And to cure this disease.

The Indy Dog Attack. 26.6.18.

(Ms Davidson's testament to the judge in the case of:
Dean Halliday and The Indy Dog Attack).

They leered and they lurched, lunging forth for my blood

Unkempt and unclean, their coats covered in mud

It was horrendous, horrific and it took all his restraint

To hold back those great hounds, m'lud, I almost felt faint.

I ran but he followed with his great savage beasts

And I couldn't help thinking, was I their next feast?

He screamed rage and anger as I begged for my life

But he just laughed and kept shouting, with obscenities rife.

My heart just kept pounding, sweat dripped from my brow

As his words echoed round me, you stupid fat cow!

Then at last I found refuge and escaped further abuse

I was free from this madman, with just my dignity bruised.

I only wish it was filmed or caught on CCTV

You'd see a typical Nationalist (and I'm sure SNP).

That's my full confession, the honest truth there m'lud

But the judge said: We saw it ya bampot an' ye're a lyin' wee fud!

The Top Rung.   3.6.18.

I've been in your fancy restaurants

Where your type must exist

I've witnessed all those functions

That humanity has missed

I have been in those cool London bars

Where the rich drink and debate,

I know about their mortgages

And each one's financial state.

Wealth has overtaken them

Their life is not their own

They're just the bankers' folly

Just messengers they've cloned

They might be human beings

They are rich with no self-worth

And those who live below them

Are condemned upon their earth.

But I see the things you hide from

And block out from your mind

You think big but miss out on life,

That part you left behind.

You swathe yourself in riches,

You're chauffeured round in cars

You dress yourself impeccably

Yet don't know who you are,

You've grown to be someone

You were never meant to be

It's time you listened to your heart

It wants to set you free.

Dumfries' 10,000.   **3.6.18.**

Have they all taken leave of their senses

Or abolished their brains

They've scratched all the sawdust away

'Til nothing remains

Old Pinney's been sold on a bribe

And moved down to Hull

But the Tories will tell you they fought it

Then get on with the cull.

We had "English for Scots" lead our rally,

What a wonderful sight

And no farmers, that I know of, joined us

But they now know we're right

Westminster's been paid by the EU

But Scots farmers await what they're owed

That's the price that you pay when The Tories

Instal their own penal code!

The Unionists came once again

Still led off by that clown

They're so proud of their Unionist rags

They were flown upside down

And we heard how his 5,000 year old Union

Pre-dated The Sphynx

But like that manky old shirt on his back

His Scots' history stinks.

Dumfries was awash with our Saltires

Against their blue skies

And the sun brought out locals to watch

Who seemed happily surprised

They witnessed a rally, the size of which,

They'd never seen

I hope they realised we were marching for them

Against all that's obscene.

The Shirt. 3.6.18.

(The Manky Shirt Brigade at Dumfries' rally).

We came across some numpties who were staunin' oan
the stairs

Ane o' them wis preachin' while the rest were sayin' their
prayers

In the shadow of Burns statue against our greatest poet's
wish

The Unionists came tae Dumfries armed again with utter
pish!

A band o' dour faces a' wi' anger in their eyes

Looked mair than jist forlorn as ten thousand passed them
by

Oh! an' ane wee wummin smiled at us wi' a look o' deep
despair

Her apologetic cringe jist said; She wanted oot o' there!

Noo, some say they were bussed in but I think they were
dragged

Three taxis wid've been enough for them an' a' their rags,

An' who is their gamely preacher who enforces unity

It seems he's clingin' tae a past where we don't want tae
be!

He blurted oot his nonsense of how he'll keep us chained

This brainless ane we call "The Shirt" is anything but sane

Ye kin forget yer Frankie Boyle, if it's real comedy ye want

Just head wi' us tae Bannockburn and you'll hear this comic's rant!

I Am You.   5.6.18.

Take me in your hand and show

The love that we both bear

Walk with me and show me off

Show them that you care

Let them see your guardian

That hovers overhead

I'm the one they lower down

In remembrance of my dead

I am the cloth of hated pride

Of innocence and gore

I am the ancient crofter

No longer on these shores

I am the one who stirs you

And fills your heart with pride

Swelling hearts and filling minds

As we walk side by side,

I'm the swathing shadow

That sweeps across the land

I'm the cloth you cling to

As passion floods your hand,

I'm the one you march with

In battle or in peace

I'm the one enveloping

The graves of our deceased,

I'm the one when you look up

Brings a smile to your face

I'm the one I'd love to see

In every dwelling place

I'm the one who feels no shame

Of a history untold

I'm the oldest one of all

More precious than your gold,

I bow down to no-one

Yet I'm no-one's enemy

I stand upright, proud and strong,

I am liberty!

I'm the cross you love to bear

And loved throughout the world

Now, let me feel this love at home,

Let this Saltire be unfurled.

For You.   **6.6.18.**

I'm glad my wealth is minimal

And my riches lie elsewhere

I am glad that I can feel alive

And not trapped by golden snares

My mind is free and not held back

By life's most unnatural threat

I've the richest friends you'll never have

And our friendship has no debt.

The Border Reivers. 7.6.18.

Ye confide in evil wi' yer son

Then tell the boy tae hush,

Oh! Tae huv a heart sae cauld

That it cannae even blush,

No' a word noo Olly

Ye must keep this tae yersel

They're only Scots for christ's sake

Let them feel oor Hell.

A bribe's afoot tae move their skills

An' London has oor back

We'll string them up like Wallace

Then pit them oan the rack

We'll rip them bare, limb fae limb

Then sack every Border town

But come, we huv nae time tae lose,

Make haste, we're London bound.

Let them protest an' fill the streets

But for them it is too late,

Be proud my son, for you and I,

Have sealed The Borders' fate.

Noo, we must move swiftly

The rest o' Scotland's next

Fae Shetland tae the Ayrshire coast

An' a' that's in betwixt,

Oor allegiance'll never be tae them

But tae them that fills oor purse

Aye, reap every harvest while ye can

An' let the rest be cursed.

Ye've made a faither proud ma son

Ye uttered no' a word

An' soon ah'll lavish wealth on ye

When the Queen knights me a lord!

Yes Clutha.　　　　　　　　**17.6.18.**
(A wee poem on Yessers partying in The Clutha).

The devil's music played fur us

As they danced wi' luggered step

A' dancin' tae their ain delight

'til through the air they leapt

Screamin' like mad banshees

Wi' demons in their heids

They danced 'til they were thrown oot

Hauf cut an' a' hauf deid.

Skirts an' kilts were swirlin'

Aboon the auld stane flair

They glided ower every inch

An' then went back fur mair

The chatterin' o' the hingers oan

An' the tappin' o' their feet

Wi' thelr glesses bangin' tables

Kept up the devil's beat

Wi' screechin' strings in highest pitch

The place fell intae mayhem

Some maddies danced a waltz wi' flags

While others danced aroon' them

Some were locked in deep debate

Wi' eyes o' drunken lords

Bletherin' through almighty slurs

Aboot some ancient wars

An' a flag wis tied tae scaffold poles

But it never raised a cheer

The gentle folk looked on in awe

An' looked at them quite queer,

While others hung 'roon tables

With stares from faraway

Chillin' wi' a smoke a drink,

Breathin' in its rich bouquet

But inside on the auld stane flair

Time wis drawin' nigh

The Outlanders who screamed an' yelled

Now sang their lullabies

Bleary eyed wi' slidin' tongues

They left coherence in the past

Their bobbin' heids bounced up an' doon,

That bounce wid be their last

Then softly, quietly, as if asleep

They gathered a' their thoughts,

Aye! That'll be right, did they hell!

They partied oan like Scots!

An' wi' glesses raised in high applause

They took the flair ance mair

Then stepped out of The Clutha

An' their new found love affair.

The Castles of The Dead.   18.6.18.

I am not guided, thankfully, by a heart that aches and yearns gold

And neither will I suffer the fool whose heart is frozen cold

For the fool who confiscates my land and proclaims it must be bare

Is the fool who acts as landlord yet seldom is he there!

He's the actor who lives out the role as a chieftain draped in robes

Then leaves with all endeavour for a life around the globe

He abandons with a fearful spite this paltry purchase claimed

And honourless is the man who would these wild highlands tame.

Thieves, rogues and vagabonds who by pomp and circumstance

Acquire by the darkest means, for it does not come by chance,

Lands purchased for a princely sum, or that which a Prince might pay,

To assume the rights of fiefdom and at their insistence, we obey.

They pontificate like an emperor aping Caesar ruling Rome

But unlike their former ruler they will never know their home

For they are the homeless in their castles where every friendship has a wage

As they walk in solace on their grounds that surround their foreign cage.

Whit's It A' Furr?   20.6.18.

We a' want somethin' oot o' life

We a' want fur the best

But it's whit we dae while we urr here

That's oor eternal test

Fur the only thing we're promised here

Is we'll a' be put tae rest

But at least a heart is beatin'

Beneath this proud auld chest.

The common man has fair few rights

The poor, nae rights at a'

They're stolen by the likes o' you

As they coorie up tae wa's

So, you define jist who we urr

Wi' some bent an' corrupt law

Sniggerin' wi' yer cronies

Giein' it a' the big guffaw!

Gollum?   22.6.18.

Her head bowed down so creepily and yet fixed her sneering eyes

Upon the great Imperialist who bade her not to rise

You snivelling little cretin, another grovelling little Brit

You may kiss the hand that governs you and will rise when I permit!

Who is this who kneels before me, who attempts to kiss my ring,

Is that the vile creature Gollum who mistakes me for her King?

Watchers. (at Bannockburn).   **26.6.18.**

A great Union beach towel's draped over a door

A baby lifted up to a window as if he knows the score!

Is this their defiance? And if so against what?

They're being trampled by London and yet blame it on Scots!

They watch as we pass them, motionless, still

But still they stand there watching, as their streets overspill,

Five thousand go past and, yes, they're still there

Just waiting and watching from behind their blank stares.

No words, no excuses, as they glare at our ranks

They're just gazing, mouths open and still firing blanks,

They're there at the start and still there at the end

Why stand and look on at something that offends?

How long can they suffer, how much pain can they take

They just stand there, and stand there, without taking a break,

Their tolerance levels must be way off the scale

And it's all self-inflicted and their stare is so stale

But their great comedy value is no myth or illusion,

We cringe cos it's real and only based on confusion.

With their rags disappearing and their numbers going down

It won't be long before Bannockburn casts its old Tory crown?

The Ventriloquist's Dummy.   29.6.18.

He really is a walloper

Full of unmeant, genial gaffes

And although it was not intentional

He gives us Scots so many laughs

But whose hand is it that guides him

Who orchestrates his moves

And while the hand is thrust up through his arse

He will never disapprove!

His face smiles gaily with a certain glee

And satisfaction fills his eyes

The swivelling head looks all around

To show off his greatest guise.

This inanimate object springs to life

And whilst devoid of human thought

He entertains his Scottish masses

And, I am told, he is a Scot.

Self-mockery with his self-attack

Are traits so highly prized

With the belief this will enhance his world

While he's actually being despised.

This self-inflicted daily ridicule

Leaves him open to attack

And this makes me wonder if he's real,

Or is this charade just all an act?

His self-congratulatory mode

And that glaikit smile he wears

Confirms there is no brain at all

In fact, there's nothing there upstairs.

Ross, you are no Lord Charles,

But your ventriloquist's no fool

To us, you're more than just a dummy

You're Scotland's biggest ever tool.

Your idiocy's incomparable,

You are out there on your own

For you're the dunce who we think worthy

To replace Murdo on that throne!

Arlene's Bigotted Bash.   1.7.18.

Arlene's here for her bigot's bash

Accompanied by her new moustache

But while preparing for her biggest splash

She sees Murdo, with his coarse panache,

Scratching wildly at his latest rash

And racist Ruth's not that abashed

As she drapes them all in an orange sash.

Feel Oor Pain.   **2.7.18.**

There's nothin' here that she's produced

A' her attacks are self-induced

Seductress or the ane seduced,

Send her hame tae roost,

Let her survey her sordid mess

Let her deny oor deep distress

Let her escape while we protest

Back tae her viper's nest.

She's the traitor wi' the killing smile

Another ane like Argyle

They're a' the same, her rank an' file

A' bitter, curt an' vile.

She does nothin' but berate

We Scots are burdens on the state

These thought oot words will seal her fate

She's the ane we rightly hate.

She wid be oor wreckin' chain

For she's the ane that stauns tae gain

Ah wish her heart could feel oor pain

As she eyes her London reign.

The Fodder That Won't Die.

We are the airways refugees

With our versions put on hold,

Where controllers hold our stories,

Where the truth is never told,

Who are we they cast aside

As if we're theirs to own?

Who are all these journalists

Whose own country they disown?

We are the bastards in their wars

The fodder that won't die

We are the power they cannot hold

The ones who will defy.

I never learnt our ancient tongue

And never knew that cost

But I've an Independent mind

And will fight for all I've lost

But bow down Scotland if you must

To all that they propose

But I'll be out there fighting

And their corruption I'll expose

When they build walls all around us

We must build a gate

Then build a bridge to rise above

Their river full of hate

For every obstacle they build

We'll rise and tear them down

For the free wheels of Caledonia

Will never stop going round.

A Thousand Tabards.

They heard all his words evaporate

Words whispered for St Peter's Gates

Words frozen and suspended for all time

Their silence is of deep despair,

An eerie hush hangs in the air,

As they bend down on one knee as though in rhyme.

Their earth holds out for Heaven's truce

A single cry, God bless The Bruce!

As a thousand loyal tabards light the land

In silence they raised up their thoughts,

Acknowledging their King of Scots

And each one looked to Heaven with clasped hands.

Towards the skies their eyes were cast

Their dying King had breathed his last

A friend knelt down and fastened down his eyes

Scotland's freedom was his aim

And gone was our eternal flame

But our greatest King, The Bruce, will never die.

As we march today on Bannockburn

Let him see his love has been returned

And fly all flags with his passion and his pride

Let London see that we are here

Show them we have cast our fear

And this time freedom will not be denied!

My People.

No matter what the verdict be

Scotland's folk have been set free

Their minds alight, their hearts afire

They'll take nae mair the London liar.

They'll question a' and mair again

'Til the common man will freely reign

O'er his thoughts and of his deeds

The risen Scot will now succeed.

The pain he felt now conquers fear

He cast one out and kept one near

And what he feels he now will say

Lest he be judged on Judgement Day.

And come that day will come his prayer

Look in his eyes and feel his stare,

He is sovereign in his ancient land,

I bow to you my common man.

Vacant Friends. 19.7.18.

For centuries they've buckled us

Wi' their warped an' twisted laws

An' still some vote these bastards in

Who further London's cause,

We've a caricature as premier

Ane o' Scotland's greatest banes

Wi' a husband takin' Trump's big bucks

Fur cagin' immigrant weans.

Her hypocrisy is there tae see

Plastered oan that gormless face

An' whit lies behind they deadened eyes

Is whit these lunatics embrace.

Ye're a' weak, submissive idiots

An' yet you think ye think yer strong

But they see ye naked, on yer knees

They've got ye right where ye belong

Yer feeble minds are vulnerable,

Ye belie a' yer beliefs

They're shafting you right in yer face

An' you gie them their relief.

You're their little prostitute

On who they a' depend

An' it's you who pulls the trigger

On the people you call friends

An' when they're a' but finished

An' you can take nae mair

It's you they'll turn that gun oan

Withoot a thought o' care.

Big Donald fae Scatland.   18.2.17.

This blond haired, blue eyed immigrant

Is Scotland's biggest shame

And anything The Bawbag does

Is not in Scotland's name

His wives are also immigrants

Yet others he will ban

For fear they're extreme terrorists

Taking over stolen land

But the terrorists have all been white

Mad gun toting Yanks,

Just Christians on a killing spree

On some modern day Crusade,

They're all white Nazi fascists

Whom their parents fought in war

But the Bawbag seems to love the things

Humans normally abhor.

You've got both eyes fixed on Trident

But you don't even have a pulse

You're dead inside, you have no soul

And, this world, you repulse.

The world and its granny

Laugh at your stupid tweets

And in every major city

They demonstrate on streets

But you can't accept that you're at fault

As you answer Lies, Lies, Lies

It's no wonder millions protest

It shows how much you are despised!

When you "come home to Scatland"

After seeing off the Bitch

You might hear some expressions

That'll leave your life enriched

But please don't visit Lewis

On another 90 second tour

Then tell us "I love Scatland"

Like some mad demented whore.

The only thing that Scotland gave you

Was your mother's tiny hands

Even relatives, with one voice,

Said you, they cannot stand,

Ye cannae even say oor country's name

Wi' that stupid Donald twang

It seems that everything ye dae

Is jist so bliddy wrang!

We know you're rich and powerful

That you've finally made the grade

Now go back to where you came from

Wi' yer US Cavalcade!

InverYess.   **30.7.18.**

I saw a host of Union flags

Though most were upside down

Held high by confused relics

Whose brains are not yet found

"If you don't like our flags" they said

"Get out our country now!"

Alarmed I was by their exclaim,

I stopped and wiped my brow.

I looked upon my friend in hand,

My Saltire, Scotland's flag

And here they were in MY country

Flying a butcher's fucking rag!

I honestly can't fathom out

Their logic or their rage

Maybe that's because there's none

When brains are disengaged!

Their eyes bulged and their veins popped out

While sweat poured down their face

And as white knuckles crushed their flagpoles

I acknowledged their disgrace

I smiled and took another step

Towards self-governance, my aim

While these British see democracy

As being shackled to their chains -

Do as we do, We OBEY

And never question why

Their logic's borne of servitude

And it's enough to make you cry.

Rusted Stones.　　　　5.8.18.

Their rusted stones cry out in pain

Some even shed a tear

And crawling down our pavements,

It's a pain I almost hear

I wish that they could take me back

To a time when all was good

Take me back to the glory days

When here, my father stood.

Today I see a pale blue sky

With nothing in between

I want to see that armoury

And be where he'd once been

I want to see the river rush

When banks were crashed by waves

I want to resurrect a time

And raise them from their graves.

I want the fire, the noise, the smoke,

The smell of molten steel

I want the children of today

To know my Clyde was real

Let the cranes and mighty ships

Thrive once more in our towns

And let the people walk with pride

And not with constant frowns.

Will we ever see their like again

Will we ever feel that pride

The rusted stones still cry in pain

As they stare down on the Clyde

It flows just like a river

But it's a river full of tears

And it's crying as it rolls along

Thinking of its better years.

When Scotland ruled the world's seas

Ships were built by men I've known

The old man and his cronies

Are now memories I own

While the tenement's tears flow slowly through

Our never-ending Clyde

They're only looking for a memory

And searching for its vanished pride.

Donalda.   **18.1.18.**

Hailed as the media's great messiah, she came to aid the BBC

She promised no more bias, no more nasty SNP

But like her predecessors, that hurdle was too great

The only thing that's progressed is the rise in all their hate!

Their reporting's non-existent and preach their master's whim

Westminster's Church still pull the strings as Lords sing out their hymns

Your backroom propaganda hasn't washed with us for years

Still, you fight against us with your lies from Project Fear.

Do they interview the Escapees, namely, Davidson, Mundell?

They're Scotland's evil caricatures, who only giggle, kiss and tell,

They quiver like the liars they are when put upon the spot

Their rage within their silence says, You Can Get Tae! That's your lot!

They never answer questions because questions aren't asked

It's a Unionist acceptance that's grown into "can't be arsed"

Your reporters wouldn't know the truth, they're all part of your regime

You're the allies of Westminster where Unionism rules supreme.

You'll never listen, never learn and the bias you create

Has caused your licences to fall and in time will seal your fate

Donalda, you're a failure and rank rotten to the core

Scotland needed you to stand but you lay down like a whore.

Civil Servants.

We give wealth to the richest which we rob from the poor

We let paedophiles roam free but jail every street whore

We're customers now for prescribed patients' drugs

But they struggle for cures and treat us like mugs

They tell us there's war on some far distant land

But can't guard nuclear bases or was that all planned?

And they want to renew them as the world is a threat

But our health, education must suffer through debt

They say we're in this together right to the end

But their comforting words are not those of friends

We're in the asylum and the crazies here rule

We are the masters yet are governed by fools!

The Betrayal and Death of William Wallace.

The pact was signed in Rutherglen's Kirk where a name would be revealed

Just another Scotsman's life betrayed, another Scot whose fate was sealed

He was captured at Robroyston by a Lord, Sir John Menteith

And the Guardian of all Scotland, no more her air he'd breathe.

In silence they dispatched the news, their riders swiftly raced

To alert King Edward Longshanks, that The Wallace was disgraced

For three long weeks, bound hands and feet, they paraded England's prize

Though anger raged within his heart, a sadness filled his eyes.

His trial, by a "foreign" court, was held at Westminster Hall

He would not bow down to England's crown nor to their cabal

And the pre-determined verdict claimed that a "traitor's" death he'd face

And at Smithfield's Haberdasher's Hall, the gallows took their place.

Chained naked to a wooden frame, he was dragged o'er cobbled stones

Pelted by what came to hand as their King took up his throne

They laid his brutal body bare, ravaged by their fun-filled day

And now he'd face his cruel death, not another word he'd say.

Hanged then dropped whilst still alive, the rope jerked his body tight

Then with joy they cut his manhood and burned them within his sight

His stomach slit then disembowelled, his entrails shown to the crowd

Then burned upon the brazier as their royalty had avowed.

The hangman held his knife aloft then opened up his chest,

And pulled out his warm, beating heart, a skill the hangman must possess

Then cut off his head and held it high for all the crowd to see

Then quartered up his body parts, all done by Royal decree.

His limbs were sent to Newcastle, to Berwick, Stirling, Perth,

The sentence for a Scottish knight for "their" treason on this earth

His head was spiked on Tower Bridge to embarrass Scotland's son

And to put the fear of Christ in Scots but that fear was all undone.

A barbaric death in barbaric times but it was a death held back for Scots

This butchery was the devil's work, another evil Royal plot

But tales of William Wallace spread and a martyr he became

And far beyond this island's realms Freedom claimed the Wallace name.

When a man stands up for his beliefs and stands up for what is right

No power can match the human faith, not even Royal might

Wallace lives in us today, in the heart of every Scot

But his Freedom is a right for all and not what we're being taught.

Beauty Sleep.   **9.8.18.**

Withered and strewn across a moor, lashed with freezing rain

They lie like death sprawled o'er stones that scatter this terrain

While the dark and moody skies above are laced with winter's sun

The shades of snow are beckoning now autumn's days are done.

The gorse and heather shed their hues, they lie a scrawny brown

And the roads that once had dusted feet, are now an icy ground,

Bent and broken are the trees that race against the wind

While rusted ochre fallen leaves have left their masters skinned.

They swirl 'round an eerie glen where life has lost its hold

Where nothing moves upon its floor as if nature lies consoled

Yet no-one comes to witness this, it sleeps, it hibernates

It's just nature's way of resting, even beauty has its traits.

And when it's fully rested we can walk back through its door

To take in all the majesty that sprawls the Highlands' moors.

YOUR Paedophilia.

They'll rape some mother's children which you choose to ignore

Then you'll vote these bastards back in power when they knock on your door

They'll wear a big rosette for you knowing your children made their bed

But you still vote these paedo lovers in, it's not your child that is dead!

Some bastards down in Westminster want a consenting age of TEN

And you're the ones who vote them in, time and time again

How sick is our society when you can't feel what those kids feel

But your compliant ignorance keeps this news from being revealed.

Hall and King and Savile are just a few that I could name

They never used a bullet but still these kids were maimed

Kids who had no justice, kids who now wish they were dead

But the BBC denied it all, it was all inside our heads.

You accepted without question the laughter of those peers

And that acceptance brought about a house of silent cheers

Some of your Lords and Ladies, ministers, who live this life so vile

Only live this mere existence because you believed that evil smile.

The Fool o' Dundee. 17.8.18.
(Manky Jaikit Man, The UKIP Refugee).

Inconspicuous they urnae

They're like the circus come tae toon

An' they'll tell ye five millennia

That this Union's been aroon'

Aye! He'll be there at oor rally

Talkin' shit an' lookin' mean

An' he'll still huv oan that manky rag

The ane that's never clean.

Vagrant shouts fae vacant minds

Wi' brains shoved up their erse

These wingin' words fae chancers

Quotin' London's chapter, verse,

The wolves have sent their sheep up here

Tae bleat their battle cries

While they stey doon in London

An' let the eejits spout their lies.

Ye'll hear them cry wi' wild romance

About how they're ridiculed

But ye jist need tae take ane look at them

An' see that they're a special kind of fool

Diz he dae this cos he's mental

Or is he seekin' some reward,

Maybe looking fur a knighthood

Tae sit wi' unelected Lords.

The Crofters' Graves.　　12.2.17.

Their empty shells surround me

The smell of life all gone

They were thrown to the darkness

And disappeared by dawn

The ships were berthed and waiting

To welcome them aboard

But the flow of tears can still be seen

From their crofts down to the shore.

You can hear the women wailing

By their broken hearted men

Farewell my bonnie highlanders

I'll no' see you again.

With their epitaphs unwritten

And their headstones never placed

Their empty crofts are coffins,

They're the graves of those displaced.

Mercenaries.   **25.8.18.**

The truth can't be uncovered when it's hidden by deceit

And funded by dark money that never have receipts,

Discretion is their ally and its silence issues fear,

Agents bound to loyalty and to codes they must adhere

They are witness to each other yet anonymous by name,

Infiltrating and then sharing, with impunity, our aims.

Thousands wave their Union flag which pays them to engage

But this loyalty they speak of is dependent on a wage,

They're social media mercenaries and paid to be controlled

And like their London masters, they're the prostitutes of gold.

Indy United.   **31.8.18.**
(The Accusations against Alex Salmond).

The accused knows not who complains

Though knows which type of crime,

It was leaked to British journalists

Who've committed him to time

With no recourse and facing fees

A crowd fund here was sought

But the British State's divisive plan

United Indy Scots.

The fatal error bullies make

By attacking just one man

Is ignoring what this man has done

For Scots in their own land

We sat, we watched, we listened

And as one our movement rose

He gave us hope, you gave us fear,

Now watch as this army grows.

But who leaked these legal papers

Was it you, The British State?

Have you looked at how the world sees you,

You're not that bloody Great!

You, in your incompetence,

Hadn't factored in Scots' pride

RIGHT NOW THIS MAN IS INNOCENT

And any guilt, courts will decide.

We will get our Independence

That will be YOUR lasting legacy

Through all your evil ways and words

It's you who'll set us free

Scotland will stand proudly

In a world you'll leave behind

You sowed the seeds that brought about

These independent minds.

Ruth's Darkest Mind.   **26.8.18.**

I've a new face every day for the many games I play

And know my friends will never do me wrong

I don't care if I'm attacked, they've always got my back

Each one bought and paid for, for a song.

When I wake up I decide if I'll be Jekyll or be Hyde

I'm the controversial package you detest

I've a labyrinth of views and I take my time to choose

Then orchestrate my friends to do their best.

If you think I've disappeared then you're a fool, I'm always here

I'm usually in the gutter with my press

And though the smell not be sweet, it's the home of our elite

Planning Scotland's turmoil and distress.

I smile each day that's dawned and laugh at how I've conned

The apathetic sheep who graze this land

Dark Money has its way of endorsing all I say

I set the price of every woman, man.

I have travelled through this land accepting all those outstretched hands

Of every sexist, racist, bigot I can find

I have ways and I have means of keeping my Dark Money clean

I'm a Tory with a cesspit for a mind.

Dark Money has a face and, in our country, has no place

Collected and then hidden by the few

They are aided by their friends who quite openly offend

The majority of Scotland's people's views.

Mitch Kilbride. A Friend to Us All.
(R.I.P. Mitch, a friend to many).

The outdoor type, a fisherman, a bagger of Munros

What else he did whilst in these hills, God could only know

Around his neck, he'd a piece of rope and from it hung his phone

A smile that would melt the hardest heart that only he could own

A friend to all who've gathered here and many more beside

The very name of, Scotland's son, belongs to Mitch Kilbride.

He climbed these hills so many times, and here, in his favourite place

We throw his ashes as he wished, and his lochan he will grace.

A journalist held in the highest esteem with a reputation to uphold

But the scripts he wrote, for all of us, were worth their weight in gold,

A real scholar and a gentleman, the most respected man I knew

And even now we're here at his request, he's still telling us what to do!

But here at last, he will be free, the pain has finally gone

And this man o' Independent mind will see Scotland's brand new dawn

Tartan blood ran through his veins, he'd a Saltire for a heart

And the hardest thing in being a friend is when you have to part.

He battled hard his whole life through, fighting just like you and me

And he hopes you'll never stop that fight until Scotland is, at last, free.

But Mitch was not a sombre man and would insist today is fun

Celebrating what he done in life and all the friendships won.

He will live on within us, he will never go away

So let's raise a toast to our friend Mitch for Independence Day.

Paul X.

No Words from This Author.   2.9.18.

She laughs at your defiance and blames you for all unrest

And she'll bastardise every honest truth, in her evil, selfish quest,

She profits from a murky world where agendas are unknown

While the bankers think their darling, has nothing to atone.

Bowing, begging, with complicit ease, she smiles her way around

The folly that is Davidson is one that's well renowned,

A book of words is all she has but to us, her silence screams

Let England have this darling while we pursue our dreams.

 We tell them but they refuse to hear and insist our words are lies

The British State is all she has for in Scotland she's despised

Accept her with our blessing but she'll have you on your knees

And you'll be left with nothing while she will set us free.

They.   **2.9.18.**

We don't hear the vendors on our streets cry out our daily news

They cry out their substitutes, ones their owners choose

But where are all the journalists, we know they're still out there

But like everyone who's in a job they've got them running scared.

Where is this democracy the merciless say exists?

It's now hidden by the golden gifts, the poor again have missed.

We will have no sense of freedom, they'll erase it from our heads

But we have shown these past few months, we're the monster that they dread

They have no sense of loyalty, their existence is their greed

They are soul-less, they are lifeless with only selfish needs

But their greed has no belonging in the world which we pursue

They've dictated long enough and any change is down to you.

A Vigil Sky.   **11.9.18**

(I was honoured to be asked to write a poem, by Dave Llewelyn, for the vigil held at Culloden Moor. I thank everyone who attended and to Karl Claridge who read it out).

I have followed this bloodstained path you took, o'er hills that you once trod

And I now stand in humble homage above your graven sod,

Hear the piper in one last sweet lament, play his forbidden air

And let the sadness fall from every note that only hope can bear.

There is no love, only death lives here, all is cold and grey

And the mist that hides two thousand graves is here again this day,

Its eerie silence haunts me yet I stand tall with Scottish pride

And the tears I feel, roll down my face, are for those who freely died.

September's vigil sky is still, and in silence, it looks down,

Down on the dead who fell that day upon this hallowed ground

And our torches tarred with blackened pitch is the light they cannot see

For here they lie, below our feet, still hoping to be free.

The cairns carry solemn plaques for those who gave their lives

And though Jacobites were crushed that day, their spirit still survives,

I stand, salute and pray for you upon this field of death

For Jacobites you always were unto your dying breath,

Lift this curse that bears them down and sweeps Culloden Moor

And let the ghosts that cannot leave be free for evermore.

I invoke the ancient spirits, rise, of all Culloden's slain,

Lift this spell they've borne so long and let no guilt there remain

But do not wrestle with your heart as you linger in your grave,

Rise and lead me in my quest and show me, what is, brave!

The pipes will guide and feed your soul and I ask that you take part

With me upon my journey and let your heart be my heart

There is so much hope, eternal, that flows through this morbid field

I beseech you join with me and I promise you no yield

For I offer all I have to give if you will only walk with me

And share in all our glory when we set our nation free.

My Ancestral Home.   **9.8.18**

Aye! Ah lived tae tell the tale for ower the seas ah've come

Where rafters reeked o' rotten ale an' oul' Tars reeked o' rum

League on league o' battered seas on a ship wi' sickly souls

An' those too sick were fed tae seas tae feed the hungry shoals.

Their Cats were rife wi' human flesh an' blood dripped aff their tails

They cut oor backs right tae the bone in this, their floatin' jail

An' ships that passed by in the night were full o' folk like me

A' shackled tae their iron chains tae stop us bein' free.

They laid oot tables fur the Lords wi' slops kept fur us below

An' they'd watch us battle fur the scraps, a' part o' their wee show

But when their corruption goes tae bed at night, it never really sleeps

Fur doon here in the battered bowels, their Cats make sure we weep.

Oh! Ah've seen yer colonial masters, the rulers of this earth

I know the price they put oan me but only I can know mah worth,

Ah've seen yer Judas many times, the kind that's bought an' sold

But ye'll find nae price upon this soul an' this heart ye'll never mould.

My heart is my ancestral home an' has been a' these years

Ah carry it around the world an' the love ah feel is fierce

I am ageless with no colour wi' a wealth they cannae own

I am rich in pride nae gold can buy an' Scotland is my throne.

I am the one who can't be bought, I am your fellow man

I am the sovereign Scot ye seek an' this here is my land.

The Truth About The Indy Girls.

They come to the rallies all smiling, promoting their wee club

And press-gang all new Members causing carnage down in the pub

Pitchers of Braveheart, their starters and food, well that can just wait

And they wonder why after six hours, they're all in a terrible state!

Rightly they're slightly quite mental, mostly deprived and depraved

For tae drink with these women at all, you'd have tae be bloody well brave

They're wild and rowdy and boisterous, which they jovially all celebrate

Then tell you their pure, honest innocence, that is their most honourable trait!

I almost believed them then thought about, a man known as "Ah Wiz There Tae"

That friend of mine's stuck in his own house, such a shame after working all day

They're out flirting with pipers and waiters and whoever lifts them off the ground

Then they've the cheek to say they're my "biatches", on which I've continually frowned!

Their detriment puts me to shame, I've a good name which I must uphold

But usually after a drink or two, I succumb and do as I'm told!

But who even are they, you ask of me, are they just lost, lonely souls?

No, these are the infamous Indy Girls and usually found out of control.

The Dream Shall Never Die.   24.9.18.

Our premier tells us she's been framed

That she's done her best and can't be blamed

And it's not just twenty seven states that laugh

The whole world's doubled up in tears

Laughing at what's happening here

But the biggest joke of all's her bloody staff.

This Union's bursting at its seams

And it keeps alive our hopes and dreams

As a man once said: The dream shall never die

We started off at forty five

And from now on they will see us thrive

Independence is coming, just say Aye!

They tell us there's no appetite

Because they know they'll lose the fight

They're feart to hold a vote they know they'll lose

And even with their paid-up trolls

They've lost every single recent poll,

Scotland's people know the path they'll choose.

If you don't stand up now and fight

You'll lose not just your human rights

They'll strip you bare of everything you own

It's their well thought-out planned mistake

And you'll soon find out it's for their sake

Because every day is theirs, you're out on loan.

Adequate Compliance.   **26.9.18.**

They want complete control of Scotland

And command of all our seas

They want our mountains, hills and glens,

They want us on our knees,

They want to seize our Saltire

Conceal our GM crops,

Change Scotch beef to British

And put Jacks in all our shops

They've commandeered our whisky

Downgraded by the rag

It'll soon be non-existent

And only sold in body bags

They want to take our country back

But kill off the Nationalists first

It seems it's not just blood they want

In their insatiable thirst!

We get what London gives us,

We get what London says,

Now they share a perfect stage

Without the slightest of dismays

They complement each other

On a pleasurable compromise

And have adequate compliance

In delivering blatant lies,

They come in different colours

But the message is the same

They have every need for Scotland

But our land must be renamed!

Heroes and Heroines of The Five Hundred.

Aye! They're battered, blistered, bruise with cuts upon their feet,

But they're full of vigour wrapped in hope where each step erodes defeat,

They are walking for awareness for our Independent cause

And in every place they come to, they are welcomed with applause.

Battling through the elements that saps their passion's powers,

They garner strength from our support, as we, from them, get ours

For they are bolstered by a great belief that spurs them on inside

And that belief is Independence and they know we're by their side.

Their inner strength, that eager will, is forged within a heart

That stands against a Union that wants our country ripped apart

But love and pain unites these hearts to give them strength to fight,

To capture steely Scots' resolve and claim our Sovereign rights.

Oh! They will let them know they're sovereign and let them know they're not alone

And that Scots will choose their future, where our choices are our own,

And these raggle taggle gypsies with their freedom bell in hand

Walk with a passion in their hearts some will never understand.

There's a pride that's beamed across this land, inspiring all who see

Scotland's sons and daughters who are friends to you and me,

They've seen the sights and heard the sounds and smelt our sweetest air,

They've paved the way for all of us, they're the storm we all will share.

Here, there are no leaders and though they may be few

They walk for me and those who can't, for freedom and for you

Yet already they're victorious though only half their miles they've trekked

So I salute these marchers proudly, they've more than earned our respect.

Worn down, they may be but for them, this walk, this quest

Is not for glorious egos or for bright medals pinned on chests

We should honour them as they've honoured us, every single name

They are our heroes, heroines and for that, have our acclaim.

?

The years could huv been kinder,

Ah think this wummin's cursed

An' let's be honest wi' oor self

She couldnae look much worse

That ruthless path she travelled

Has found its rightful place

It seems they etched that road map out

Upon her fearsome face.

I saw her on the telly

An' before she even spoke

Ah felt masel churn up inside

An' made me want tae boak

Ah cannae bear tae watch her

She's evil tae the core

Is she Auld Nick here in disguise

Or jist the devil's spore?

Whit kind o' Christian wummin

Takes food aff children's plates

It's nae wonder naeb'dy likes her

She brings on all this hate

Ah'm glad ah'm oot o' England

An' where ah want tae be

 There's only ane ane thing wrang wi' here

Oor Scotland is nae free.

The Forgotten.

They don't hear the madness or suffer the screams

As the dying fade on from their lost hopes and dreams

They're living outside staring at silver beams

In an old cardboard box that's burst at the seams.

You Never Won My Heart.   **27.9.18.**

There's a vow I must uphold and that's why this heart is so cold

I don't think my love was ever meant for you

There is no love just remorse, every move I made was forced

So I'm ending this as lovers often do.

It was hell instead of bliss as though I don't exist

So I blocked you from a mind you tried to own

You said we'd be secure but I was just your lonely whore,

Now I think it's time to go alone.

You never see my friends, your life's one big pretence

Sucking up to people that you hate

But it's your friends who're the clowns with empty words they bring on down

While boasting to the world that they're still great.

It's been so long since we've been friends, now our time is at an end

Our thoughts are now a million miles apart

As we say our last goodbyes, don't hit me with your lies

And still you wonder why you never won my heart!

My Bond of Trust.   25th September 2018.

Words are a' ye need fae me

Nae scrievin' will ah gie

An' if mah word isnae guid enough

Then neither's yours fur me.

Christianity According to Theresa May.

She falters to worship and feigns a wry, sadistic smile,

Expecting her god to make her time worthwhile:

I bow down to no-one and do as I please

You bow to me, you get on your knees

For if I cleanse your earth showing meagre restraint

Then you will pardon my killings and make me a saint!

(An intro to the rally from the pavements of Edinburgh).

We traded smiles and kisses, every stranger was my friend

I looked down on The Sovereign Mile and saw blue from end to end

They snaked around the castle walls and stepped on every stone

No one here was a burden and no-one was alone…..

Auld Reekie's Rally.   27.9.18.

Tae Caledonia's capital, tae Edinburgh we'll go

An' see oor nation's finest in her greatest ever show

We'll funnel through the tap o' it, at the church o' auld St Giles

An' dae a dance a' doon that hill they ca' The Royal Mile.

Friends will jostle tae be found but others they will find

Where narrow streets are thick an' fast wi' Independent minds

We will march right down The Mile an' end up in oor park

An' fifty thousand picnics will be there 'til well efter it's dark.

There'll be nae stalls or stagin' cos we're told they're no' allowed

But we'll no' be like the sheepish anes, oor voices will be loud

We'll be laughin', tellin' stories an' prob'ly huv a drink or two

An' that's somethin' we excel at, dis that no' appeal tae you?

If ye want tae come an' join us, ah'm sure ye'll huv some fun

A day oot in yer capital but ah cannae promise ye the sun

Bring yer flags an' banners, yer dugs an' a' yer weans

But maistly get yersel here tae free us fae these chains.

My Wee Blue Enamelled YES Badge. 2.11.16.

I've a wee enamelled badge I wear

And I wear it with great pride

And I think of all you thousands

Who stand proudly by my side

It's just a simple badge and message

But it shouts out loud to me,

My wee blue enamelled YES badge

That says Scotland will be free.

When I see the flags, all flying high,

In the Square or in The Green

Or anywhere my friends are

It's the best sight to be seen

When they dress up in their tartans

Even in their finest highland dress

I look with pride on all of them

And my wee badge saying YES.

No matter what my jacket is

My badge takes pride of place

And walking down the street I see

A stranger's smiling face,

I know just why they're smiling

And I know it's not for me

It's for my blue enamelled Yes badge

That says set our Scotland free.

To some it's insignificant

But to me it means the world

It signifies just who I am

As I watch our flags unfurled

This wee blue enamelled badge I wear

Brings back memories for me

But one day I'll look for one last time,

And that's the day that Scotland's free.

They say we are inclusive

And who am I to disagree

It's a symbol of my passion

That no man can take from me

It's just a wee blue enamelled Yes badge

Given to me by a friend

It's a badge that says we've had enough

And that London's rule must end.

This is not a badge of protest

Against any other race or man

But it is against Westminster

Who are destroying this, my land,

We see their hatred coming

But the blind refuse to see

Stand up and take your country back

Be proud, make Scotland free.

Our First Minister.   5.6.18.

Oor FM's pure dead brilliant an' gets called a' sorts o'
names

She's jist oot there lapping up her walks an' playing a'
kinds o' games

She disnae need her minders or the hassle that they bring

She's happy openin' up a park then playing oan the swings.

She's ane o' us an' loves it, giein' selfies wi' the weans

Kissin', cuddlin', haudin' them as if they were her ain

She disnae dae refusals even when she needs a rest

She sees the crowds as right good pals an' no' as bloody
pests!

A' the wummin coorie roon' while their men a' kinda hide

But they're smilin' fae a corner and burstin' oot wi' pride,

It disnae matter who ye urr, she wullnae pass ye by

Oan the streets or in a shoap or runnin' through the rye!

Ah huvnae met oor FM but heard she's goat a heart o' gold

Ah only know this through some pals o' mine an' the
stories ah've been told

But croass her and ye'll get a tongue that'll make ye want
tae greet

An' she'll answer a' yer questions even when she feels dead beat!

There urnae many country's leaders who love tae meet the likes o' us

Fae private jets tae first class trains, she even jumps the bus

Ah said before she's ane o' us an' long may this queen reign

Jist keep daein' whit ye dae the noo an' we'll vote ye in again.

Gorgeous Galloway.

My name is Gorgeous Galloway and my time on this earth

Will always be defined by cash, my friend's all know my worth

My allegiance as a rebel is to The Union and The Crown

And I'm open to all offers that will help keep Scotland down.

I was once a socialist who saw Farage as Britain's curse

But now I see him as a friend and one who swells my purse.

Hammond's Self-Superiority.   **6.11.18.**

Is it arrogance that strides the floor with each step full of contempt

Or is it with hoi polloi's dark disregard, this man thinks himself exempt

From the mediocre courtesy that respect is shown to fellow peers

But no, this bastard boldly strolls right past, encouraging Scottish jeers.

What ails the mind of such a man that would so wilfully enrage

And exile a neighbouring nation with whom he refuses to engage

But yet affords himself a piety blessed with his English pompous pride

That lets this self-superiority cast all that Scotland boasts aside.

In his eyes, we are nothing, not even worth his measly glance

He passes saying nothing, all by intention, not by chance

But what kind of man demeans a race and brings on such disgrace?

A man who's filled with hatred and knows that hatred has its place!

Their benches pander to this hatred, their jeers drown out our voice

And this Brexit farce that Scotland's in, is not by our but England's choice

Only their numbers overpower us for it is certainly not their brains

But their insistence to proceed with it now renders Westminster, quite insane.

Feed The Beast.   9.11.18.

They paint a dire picture and explain they're doing their best

But the reality is so much worse yet you block out all protest,

They feed you their incompetence and tell you it's their treat

Then present you with a voucher so your working family can eat.

This unrelenting drive for chaos damns everyone, yes, all

Where the victim is the victor and sadly cheers his own downfall,

They are normalising crises way beyond our weirdest dreams

And these educated halfwits will incite you to extremes

For these people have no morals, they are people in the loosest sense

And though you feel their cruel wrath you will jump to their defence

Because you have reasons, dire, dark and cruel, underhand

And inflict upon the rest of us, this darkness in our lands.

It's a necessity which you hold dear with a belief you don't believe,

A refusal to see with honest eyes your friends who daily grieve

You afforded them your paltry coin as they took away your life

And that foolish pride and selfishness has plunged, in you, its knife

They believe in only them and that lifestyle that you gave

Do you think they'll shed a tear for you as the sod's poured on your grave?

Raab and even Thicker People.   9.11.18.

Ah, who would be a Tory, they're all jumped up little pricks

And daily they outdo themselves trying to be the biggest dick

It's a contest they all relish where ignorance heads the

Queue

And the arrogant in second place have joined just for you!

Yet these pompous righteous bastards render us the ones insane

While shite pours out their mealy mouths fed by their half a brain

Is Raab the weirdest of them all, whose words and mouth are out of sync

He can't even spell his name and seemingly, never taught to think!

Did you know we're on an island? Well, that came as a shock to him

And don't even mention trade deals, he dismissed them on a whim!

This embarrassment speaks for all of us as we shudder in disgrace

But it's not just him, it's all of them, they're all a waste of space

And then they say that we should trust them and put our differences aside

While they're ridiculed by the wider world you can see them squirm inside

I can't even watch them now, they just disgust and sicken me

And the best of all our options, is to set our nation free.

The Houses.   18.11.18.

In its grand foreboding entrance, they're in awe and stand aghast

At a greatness that's a mere facade built on relics from its past.

The imposing building bearing down is filled with carvings so ornate

While the statues are divided between the hated and the great,

Where debates of lovers hover in the halls that hold the right

Where blood has stained the world o'er of enthused Empirical might.

Its history is a bludgeoned path, conquering by divisive rule

Where two houses once admired are only acknowledged now by fools

For the fool is one who will not learn and ignores the pleas of peers

Where even gargoyles close their Gothic eyes and cringe at what they hear.

Our Scottish Brand. 18.11.18.

Senselessly they beat themselves

As they watch their food rot on their shelves

They're trying to get their Empire back on track

But their business plan was not thought through

And now they're fucked what do they do

As all that's left is produce with a Jack!

Battered, beaten, they know they've lost

But refuse admission of that cost

Defiantly and stubbornly soldiering on

They scratch heads at their demise

As profits drop and losses rise

And they waken every day to starker dawns.

As the Union forces us away

Their mood grows darker every day

Still clinging to a flag that splits our land

Take off that Jack and cut your loss

And replace it with our St Andrew's Cross

You're in our country, keep the Scottish brand.

Are you frightened there might come a day

When we will rise and we will say

That Scotland's fed up with your Union taunts

For as Scots with Independent powers

We will succeed and promote what's ours

And ensure that Scotland gets what Scotland wants.

Andrew William Stevenson Marr.   **18.11.18.**

I am a warring journalist, bruised and battle scarred

I put women in their place, my name is Andrew Marr

I hassle prominent women and refuse them all debate

They're pumped up clerks with bras on and deserving of my hate!

They come on here with skirts and legs and plaster on their face

But I'm the little sanctimonious prick who'll put them in their place

I'm the condescending type and I'll patronise at will

For to see a woman cower and cry, gives me the greatest thrill.

I'm backed by those who understand and who're complicit in my rage

What right have women on this show who don't see me a sage

For thirteen years I've entertained with these playthings on my show

They're only good for one thing, and that, I'm sure you know.

I deal with Sturgeon, Queen of Scots and that bampot Theresa May

But just who the hell do they think they are, over-riding what I say

Does no-one her care how I feel, do you think it fair and just

They deserve my every crass remark, they fill me with disgust!

I'm a complete and utter bastard, a bully and a cad

I'm the Scots born Tory boy, I am Glasgow's Sir Galahad

My abusiveness to women is a trait I that I hold dear

I'm the one with balls here, I hope I've made that clear!

Truly Meant Good Wishes.   17.11.18.

I really wish you success

As you clean up your mess,

We've decided to go our own way

As we say our goodbyes

There'll be tears in my eyes

But they won't be the tears of dismay!

This Land. 16.11.18.

My land, your land, our land, this land,

Where most here were born and raised

Is a land to be so very proud of,

A land which her children should praise

And those who condemn it should fire up a rage

That burns right into our souls

These are the people whose only great worth

Is bowing down to outsiders' controls.

We have given so much yet get so little back,

Only acknowledged for things we don't do

We deserve our own voice and our government of choice

It's coming but that's down to you

And though some are against us more stand by our side,

They see what our future can hold

Some see us a faction, a cult, a wee gang,

But our future is not based on gold.

That's all they're after, that's all they want,

A full belly filled up with their greed

These righteous and pompous self-caring souls

Don't care what the people here need!

Their type of success is a harrowing embrace

Enveloped around their black hearts

Theirs is a culture that all Scots must reject

And it's a culture where we have no part.

I Seek no Permission.   19.11.18.

I neither seek permission or allowance of your grant

Nor waste my time upon your will whene'er you say I can't

You think me buckled to your chains, but, alas, you'll find I'm not

You have no sovereignty o'er me nor any other Scot.

This parity you boast of comes begging on our knees

And your pride is a construction, built only on disease

But I do not bow, I am no slave yet am bound by slavish rules

Where superiors crave injustice executed by your fools.

There is no fairness in this war you've waged against the poor

You can't even show compassion when their deaths lay at your door,

Do you believe a word you say? Do you believe your lies?

Even when we criticise them, you don't even act surprised!

Because deaths to you come easily, you can't even show remorse

You can't even manage false tears for the deaths that you endorsed

Your finery's of no consequence, your arrogance bears no pride

But your tongue is the betrayal which no fancy suit can hide.

Are fancy words and rhetoric all that your people have to cheer?

If so, I pity all your ilk when you hold their lives by your fear

But the whistle has been blown, we are ready, standing by

To say farewell to our dependency, Independence now is nigh!

Yon Maister.

Wid they no' rip the heart oot ae enthin's that grand

They'd sell oot their ain sister at yon maister's command

Then scream oot blue murder if somethin' went wrang

Time tae get the fuck oot, we've been wi' them too lang.

You Never Will Be Free.   **19.11.18.**

I saw him once and not again, down by the sheltered tree

Slouched over in the night beside his bed

Tonight was calm, at least for now,

As he turned to me and said

It's you my friend, I'm sorry for, you never will be free.

I've travelled life's rich highways but all roads have to end

Don't spare a thought for those as old as me

But think of all the young ones, they're just the same as
you

It's them my friend, I'm sorry for, they never will be free.

Your neck is hanging in a noose with chains around your feet

It's the slavery that you're too blind to see

The cost to them is nothing, you made them all yourselves

It's all of you, I'm sorry for, you never will be free.

I'll pass you in the morning and wave as I go by

As I leave the shelter of my tree

Freedom is that refugee that lives inside your head

Freedom of the mind is when you're free.

The Sturgeonator.   **19.11.18.**

For rats and weasels, snakes and moles and any other kind of traitor

Or when all seems lost and talks break down, she'll be your mediator

No jobs too big, no jobs too small but first you must locate her

Just dial Brexit 999 and ask for The Sturgeonator.

Wee Nicola. 22.11.18.

Born in Dreghorn's summer

In the county of auld Ayr,

A lass who wis tae realise

Her greatest love affair.

A' dressed up in her leathers

Wi' a mullet on her heid

She sharpened up that little mind

Determined tae succeed

So she pogoed up the dancin'

An' danced tae her ain choons

An' though the Thatcher ane is deid

She must be birlin' roon'

Furr withoot auld Maggie's hatred

Some say she widnae be

The Nicola that we a' love

Queen of the SNP.

The Cowering Rat.   23.11.18.

Trawling through back alleys

Shuffling without care

He cowers like a wandering rat

And sniffs the dank, damp air,

Eyes flit nervously, side to side,

Leering, twitching, eyes,

As the sleekit, snivelling liar

Seeks out the traitor's prize.

Uneasily he moves along

In agitated state,

A figure of immorality

With his denials now in spate,

Discourteous and disloyal

He's after siller groats

Traipsing on through darkened lanes

Seeking out the traitor's note.

Honour. **25.11.18.**

As they bask in the moonlight with brandies

And reach for their Havana cigars

They look down on you through smeared windows

In some poky wee hole called a bar.

They'll guide to make you feel guilty

'Til you're nothing in honour or name

And they'll seize every asset you give them

Then leave you with all of the blame.

When the fault of another is questioned

And the words of our own aren't heard

They are carried away by a jury

Orchestrated by some missing laird.

Well he makes all his false accusations

And screams at the absent defense

He blames every Scotsman he's known,

Backed up by the jury's pretence.

What's wrong with the people of Scotland

They have powers beyond our control

As you pick up the scraps from their table,

They're picking your pockets of gold.

The Brexit Trawler.   25.11.18.

She had won but we lost

And it was all at our cost

As we watched the boat crash o'er the waves

Then she signalled that smile

One that's never worthwhile

And sent Scottish fish to their graves.

Parts One & Two.   27.11.18.

For Brexit and England,

They storm forth in debate

And use their powers democracy

To unite their bond of hate.

This bent o'er vile Christian

The high priestess of wealth

And the poor man's weak messiah

Who'll try victory by stealth

Will take the stage for nothing more

Than to further their own aims

For who'll benefit from these debates

When both are just the same?

They're here tae sell their souls tae us,

Anes they've a'ready selt

It's time that a' o' Scotland

Got these two bloody telt

But where is yon wee lassie,

Is it likely that they're feart

Well, maybe, if they let her oan

They'll get their arses seart!

She's the answer, she's a plan

An' listens good as well

But these two bampots need locked up

In their democratic Hell!

The Russian Front in Scotland.   28.11.18.

You vilify Russian "friendly foes" because of dirty tricks

Beating and berating them with your hypocritical stick

But you're the same as Putin, blocking out free speech and press

There'll be no-one there who'll criticise the questions you address.

As you tour the isles of Britain, you'll dictate who will be there

To welcome you, to question you, this to you, is reasoned, fair

And still you seek to close us down with independent voices banned

Even knowing your quest has floundered and your control's lost all command.

Where was the speech Ms Sturgeon made, our voice of unity

It wasn't on our state run news but on Russia's state run, RT.

You think you hold our nation back but in truth you help our cause

You still refuse to listen and, in foreign courts, fight our Scots laws

What do you fear apart from truths, is it a future without you

Or is it someone helping with your debts, debts which you've accrued?

The Answer.   30.11.18.

Out of all Scottish questions,

There is one that hits me, Why?

So I asked some fervent patrons

What's that strange flag you fly?

That's our national flag son,

Aye! It's a sight that is rare

But it seems maist o' Scotland

Don't want it oot there,

D'ye know it's banned in some pubs,

Aye! Oor ain national flag

Ah Know, it's bloody disgusting son

But ye'll get in wi' the rag.

Oors are hidden in hooses

In cupboards an' in drawers

A' tucked away neatly

Or hung up behind doors

It's so unpatriotic

I jist don't understand

Whit's wrang wi' this nation

Whit's wrang wi' this land,

They should be up their oan flagpoles

Soarin' high wi' oor pride

Tae mirror oor spirit

That's too often denied

It should be flown from castles

An' Hooses o' State

Instead o' that apron

Which maist o' us hate.

Aye! The night they'll a' party

Wi' their jigs and their reels

An' no giein a damn

How the rest o' us feel

They're here furr a weekend

An' pit oan oor warpaint

No' carin' aboot Scotland

Or Saint Andrew, oor Saint.

It should be The Saltire

That's up there flying high

No' the flag o' a Union

That drips blood fae the sky

An' oan this day of a' days

This, Saint Andrew's Day

We should a' toast his Cross

The true Scottish way.

Saint Andrew's Night.   30.11.18.

Urr yeez a' oot gallovantin' wi' partyin' in mind

Dancin', laughin', huvvin fun an' drinkin' 'til ye're blind

But when ye're a' up giein' it laldy, spare a little thought

Fur the poor, unfortunate others who wid love tae be a Scot.

Some Fight For Nothing, They Fight For Less.
1.12.18.

People scream but they're disowned

The Leaders say they'll go it alone

The powers that be are fighting to be free

With the greatest brains they delve

Into plans they soon will shelve

It's a war where no-one sees their dignity

They lash themselves in bitter chains

A battered Unit's their remains

The odds against them now are truly stacked!

They manoeuvre swiftly to outflank

But remember they're just firing blanks

Now they say defense is their best plan of attack!

Cut to ribbons torn and frayed

Outmanoeuvred and outplayed

Then reach the border where they draw the line

But they don't know who's friend or foe

In a land they wish they'd got to know

Ignorance is bliss, they'll be just fine.

Back on the mainland there's civil unrest

From North and South and East to West

With Rebel factions trying to stop this war

The powers came out ill-prepared

They're backing down and running scared

What's the point? What are they fighting for?

With the darkness falling down

They creep back discreetly underground

Then summon all their allies to their side

But with all their friends saying No!

They've no Plan B, nowhere else to go

They're committed to a deal of suicide!

LOOK!   *2.12.18*

How many people must we see die

Before we notice their plight?

How many people must we walk by

Before they give up the fight?

How many more like them

Must we put in a grave

What help have you offered?

Is enough all you gave?

Empirical Chains.

You cling to a greatness

That was absorbed in the past

You're the steadfast portrayal

Of your empirical class

But there's nothing to garner

Because nothing remains

And if you're not too impatient

We'll give you back your chains.

Get Out!   3.12.18.

They once came from all over

Like bold pioneers

From Portsmouth to Partick

They were all welcomed here

To flourish and prosper

For both of our sakes

Now some wish they hadn't

Made their greatest mistake.

They've been wrongly accused,

Abused and refused

Their right to live with us,

They've been bloody well used

By the racists and bigots

Who govern these lands

They're not thanked but embarrassed

And deported first hand.

We don't need their input

Or their vast expertise

Yet they all see our countries

Are down on their knees

We've lost families, neighbours,

Some partners and friends

And there's no sign of this stopping

And no chance of an end.

While our bigoted masters

Scuttle round on all fours

They still manage to send

Damning letters through doors

We've considered our options

And you cannot stay

You're being deported

And you have no say!

Our scales of injustice

Are not fit for our needs

They're biased and weighted

To a colour and creed

If you're rich, white and Christian

Like that heretic May

She might even sign it,

I hope you have a good day!

Vile Bastards.   **3.12.18.**

I've been troubled by the greatness of the gracious
Kirstene Hair,

This blue eyed blonde from Brechin has views she loves to
share

And the only sound from that empty head is her
nauseating sigh.

As it seeks self-praise from colleagues whose brains have
been bled dry.

Now, Ross Thomson's not the brightest spark but they're
both of the same mind

The dumb blonde and the glaikit one have never had a
brain assigned

But they seem to be the perfect pair and they'll probably
never part

They're just like all the other criminals, tearing the
poorest's worlds apart.

These two are heartless bastards who pose in stores with
beaming smiles

Alerting us to Foodbanks, they've forced upon these British
Isles

And now they stand there with their owners, so proud of
what they've done

In a battle where the wealthy laugh while the poor are being undone.

It's a travesty, deplorable and yet they're locked in self-esteem

Praising all their British policies and killing more than just a dream.

The Contemptuous Trial. 4.12.18.

You strolled in like a queen

In your usual disgrace

Every movement was noticed

Every smile was misplaced

You heard all the whispers

As you searched round with eyes,

You have only just realised

How much you're despised.

Your heart should be heavy

But Alas! It is light

Uncaring, unfeeling

As you rise now to fight

But you're standing alone

And the charge is contempt,

You now face your accusers

Yet still think you're exempt.

Your nerves are erratic

Your speech is subdued

As the noise from the benches

Grow ever more lewd

They've abandoned you, left you

And gone are the cheers

They're now baying for blood,

You've been killed by your peers.

The Speaker now stands

And the black cap is raised

The House stares in discomfort

All smiles are erased

And his solemn face echoes

The sentence he'll serve,

No compassion is shown

She got what she deserved!

Oh! But these are the words

Of the outcome we seek

It's a crime we are lied to

And the havoc they wreak

For in this House with no logic

All failings are hailed

And the guilty walk free

When they all should be jailed.

Guiltless.   **12.12.18**

As she sits upon the cold stone steps, she sees us pass her by

Unknowing and unwilling to ask the question, why?

She is young, a doctor, and trained to save our lives

Now she's asking us to help, she is begging to survive.

We have seen them huddled, talking, but refused to hear their words

But we always listened to her as she walked among our wards

Now she's a lonely, unkempt figure with a mindset slightly bruised

But we judged her with our glancing eyes, she's already been accused!

Scots' Tirades. 12.12.18.

They love to criticise my ways

And my Golum-esque weird stance

They scandalise my wealthy garb

And slate me when I dance

My smile is not my shining light

And the years have not been kind

I must've run so fast going through that rye

I left my brains behind

But I've done my best, I swear to God,

I do my damnedest to compete

Though competence does not equate

To the fervour that I mete

I am hopeless, I get locked in cars

And need assistance from my aides

It seems misfortune follows me

Just like these bloody Scots' tirades!

Shooting Ourselves.   **13.12.18**

They gathered on beaches, dug in on the dunes

As they sang their archaic war tunes

Their rifles were primed as tanks rolled the sand

They were here to take back their land.

As they looked out to sea, there was nothing to see

Yet insisted they would fight to be free

But in their pitiful plight, they found no foe to fight

While demanding a war was their right.

We must have a war, who cares what it's for

(They salivate like great Labradors)

For right here on these shores, tempered hearts will be forged,

We're here for the Empire by George!

They fired their guns while their brains were undone

Mammy, Daddy, what the fuck have we done?

I then looked at myself and the further I delved

That's when I saw us all shooting ourselves.

Complicity of Royal Assent.　　　**15.12.18.**

Why do you stride with gallus pride

When they've made your life a mess

Why do you hide behind the snide

When they pour on you this stress?

They demand, they command,

They determine Scotland's fate

We have no friends so fear the end

Within this corporate State

And fear the queen, whose act, obscene

Was complicit in their cause

Her royal assent has only meant

She cares not for our laws.

Beautiful Sadness. **15.12.18.**

I'm in love with her beauty and splendour

And get lost in her mountains and glens

But when night comes, it's then I surrender

And dream her all over again.

With isles disappearing at sunset

Then arising in bluest of seas

They float with the relics of castles

Like a dream that's caught up in a breeze.

Not all our roads lead to another

Some nestle where nowhere is found

And the sweetest song ever remembered

Is when there is never a sound.

Our past may be shaded from glory

And riches unjustly shared

But treasures abound in this country,

Found in the warmth of a people who care.

It is here I will rest when my time comes

In this land where I was born

She has given me all that I ask for

And yet, still leaves me forlorn.

She holds me as I share in her fortune

And there's no other place I would be

But I hear in her voice, a sadness,

She is still crying out to be free.

Narnia.   15.12.18.

There's nae lion, they've a witch but nae wardrobe

An' they'll tell you that Narnia exists

But their Party's renowned for their cokeheids

An' ah'm sure they're a' fleein' an' no' pissed.

The Feared.   15.12.18.

You gave me your fear, I cast it aside

My land gave me hope which I still keep inside

I sought out the truth when you offered me lies

And yet you still wonder why you're so despised!

Your imaginary benevolence is a deceit you impart

And its cruel injustice cuts through this heart,

Your words run on empty as your world disappears

And the only truth now is you have nothing but fear.

It's our resources you need and you will not be content

Until your raping's exhausted and every last penny spent

Only then will you leave us and consider us free

When you have all you want and all you want to be.

Gallantry In Treachery.   16.12.18.

These wounds o' oors are deep an' raw

An' a' shamelessly designed

But the pain is so much harsher

When it festers in the mind.

We knew the game but not their rules

An' he embraced oor pain

An' official who presides up here

Assisted in their gain.

Aye ! The Rat of Holyrood

Expressed his Union's views

An' knew damn well he sold us out

An' delay would see us lose.

Starkest is that absent love

So false that fondest kiss

They chain us up and leave us cold

Before we're tossed 'to their abyss.

His gallantry's in his treachery,

He played Westminster's game

An' knew he handed over Scotland

Yet felt nae bloody shame.

The Blanket.   **17.12.18**

The nameless ones peer through eyes

Where death is sent to rest

Their dingy hideouts, coveted,

By a mind that's now possessed,

The etchings of a weary face

Is where trust must not take hold

Their stories stay within them,

They are stories seldom told.

You chastise them and who they are

Never knowing who they were

You amble down your busy street

Then quicken in despair

Passed the dregs, the lowly scum

Who are not worth your time

And only see them in their failings

Bickering in medieval mime.

These peasants who revolt you

Sprawl beneath a gilded door,

Showing half their body's flesh

To the window dresser's store,

Their hand gripped to a paper cup

That has seen much better days

By the twitching body, still alive,

And peering through a glaze.

He's where he doesn't want to be

And twists himself around,

He has had enough of people

And crawls back in the ground,

His forehead's the unseen tattoo

Which everyone has read

He's the one we do not see

Yet notice all his beds.

He's the one who troubles us

Yet he's the worried man

He's the one who's kicked and punched

But too frail to raise a hand

Yet you turn with fear upon your face

But he's the frightened one

You are all so close to being him,

Yet you think you have won.

He's the blanket refugee

You've been told, don't go near

But he's the man who once was you,

Please smile and ease his fear. X

Hooray! We Won!   19.12.18.

Look, here come the real abusers

With their British stranglehold

Forfeiting love of family

So their country can be sold.

See the Brexit soldiers marching

Backed up by their tanks and guns

Barricades on every corner

Move and you'll get fucking done!

Come the night and come their curfew

Searchlights shine on every street

Come outside and find our welcome

Is not the one you'd like to meet.

Strikers rights are now abolished

Any pickets will be shot

Scabs will all be well rewarded

Said not any decent Scot!

Please remember when out shopping

Ration books can't buy you beer

Prohibition's now upon us

Any found, they'll commandeer!

We don't need your immigration

We can work and feed ourselves

But all they find with their free coupons

Are empty shops with empty shelves.

There's no prescriptive medication

Hospitals count out their deceased

They're only stockpiling guns and bullets

And bombs meant for the Middle-East.

Destitute, now cold and hungry

No jobs, prospects and no life

Oh! But just to have our freedom

Is that not worth all this strife?

Fracking's poisoned all our waters

Cholera is on the rise

But here's the Corporal with his Punishment

Saying no-one really dies!

Change the border, change the border,

Rampant is the British cry

We're the masters of that colony,

Move those Jocks all up to Skye!

Hear the British people cheering

Hooray! We have won our fight

Fuck your European Union

And fuck off with your human rights!

Lord Soames.   **20.12.18.**

(Described by one ex-lover as "like having a wardrobe fall
on you with the key still in").

We have heard his quips and famed remarks

And, in the past, of his sexual prowess

A man who knew not of his feet,

Even when he was undressed,

Once the largest man in Christendom

He has shed shitloads of weight

And I have to say, with honesty,

He still looks a bloody state.

This, accused, sexual harasser dwells

Where they don't question what he says

And he enjoys the detriment received

And clearly cares not for his prey.

He bears malice without prejudice

And gender has no hiding place

Where smugness wraps around the wrinkles

On that ever lengthening face.

He has that annoying pompous trait

That aristocrats hold dear

But to be an old Etonian too

Commands exemption from his peers.

He is truly his grandfather's grandson,

Derisory and absurd,

Humiliating and contemptible

With his ever flippant words.

Still They Do Not Listen.   **20.12.18.**

Patience has no place in here but yet, patiently they wait

While others jump and fall like flies to decide upon our fate.

They continue with their vile jibes and tell us they know best

'til the menagerie has quietened and the animals lay to rest.

As our Members rise to speak, others rise to leave the hall

Their voice echoes in a wilderness where no-one hears their call

Jeers replace the great Hurrahs! with sneers replacing japes

From the sanctimonious benches filled with these soured Jackanapes.

Those who stay to mock their words never hear what being said

While some reflect on victories, disrespecting all our dead

But they're only here to heckle and to drown out Scotland's voice

This was the voice of reason but has descended to a noise.

The insanity of their vanity means that England always rules

We are disregarded and disgraced by these utterances of fools

We are rebellious in our ways as we buck their deathly trend

And yet they will not listen to the nation they call friends

Who can hear the Scottish voice in the midst of your affray

Keep this up Westminster and it will be Scotland walking away!

Our Political Banking Game.   21.12.18.

We are the Corporate Bankers,

We are our guarantors

And we're always here to bail us out

That's what your money's for.

In here is a Community,

We're one and all the same,

Your poverty's making us all rich,

Yet you'll never see us shamed.

We rely upon the homeless too,

No address, no claim

But guess who gets the money

And we don't even need your name!

We're involved in everything

And pay no Corporate Tax

We own the Inland Revenue

And scratch each other's backs.

We make the laws with loopholes,

Ones we'll never close

And all those Virgin contracts

Were never being opposed

Remember that we need you

Your vote is paramount

And that wee cross is all we need

To swell our bank accounts

Last of all and best of all,

We're the funders of all wars

We are the bankers' syndicate,

You know who you're fighting for!

Bloody Immigrants!   **22.12.18.**

They want immigrants deported and only whites here
should remain

I question if they've thought it through or even if they have
a brain.

You know the lazy, idle layabouts who prop up every bar

The ones who're far too ill to work but fill our streets with
cars

But who will be the bouncers that mind doors at all their
clubs

Who will serve these shirkers drinks as they languish in
their pubs

And who will man the bookies when they stagger to place
bets

But these immigrants will be blamed when their winnings
turn to debt.

Who will sign their doctor's line when they fake that they
are ill

And who will then dispense for them their bitter little pills?

Where are the white drivers of their taxis, buses, trains

And when they go on holiday who'll be the pilots of their
planes?

Who are all the hotel staff, the cleaners, chambermaids

The kitchen staff and waitresses whom they pleasurably degrade?

Who will clean their mess up and neatly make their bed

'Til they come back and curse them then rest their drunken head,

Listening to your favourite songs that don't always strike white chords

They don't even get the irony of black emancipated words.

They've even got a shade of white that's purest by its tongue

An accent that will bring a smile till racist songs are sung,

Their football, rugby, cricket teams are packed with non-white stars

But there's no mention of a colour, creed when spoken of in bars,

They idolise them in their songs and punch the air with sweet content

But they never really meant these guys, it's the other ones they meant!

I have given all the empathy their racist bigotry deserves

I have listened and dissected all they think they have observed

But this endemic apathy is all these bitter minds have ever owned

A festered mind through hatred is all they may have known

But in this queer Utopian quest, and it's one that's based on hate,

in their eyes, is the only way, to make their Britain Great.

UFO. Unseen Flying Objects.   **23.12.18.**

There was no volcanic ash today, no tornadoes or cyclones

But it was a day when all intelligence were outdone by unseen drones

It's the latest sci-fi blockbuster and it's been totally miscast

Reminiscent of the silver screen's B Movies of the past.

It Is targeting an airport swooping over sovereign skies

It's the latest of these stealth machines, unseen by naked eyes,

Planes are grounded, people stranded, planned holidays delayed

All this by a Government, some say, a game's being played.

But it's the absurdity of Britain that's facing these alien attacks

And it seems there are no answers, not even questions asked!

Our technologies are helpless but barking dogs can take them down

Said a Tory from her circus act by orders from her chief of clowns.

We can fly men to the moon and satellites can scan our eyes

But These unseen flying objects has got a nation paralysed!

But these drones could have been Martians, then, would our world survive

Or did Enid Blyton choreograph it all with The Famous MI5

It's Christmas time, it's pantomime, where nothing's as it seems

With UFO's in starring roles in the great Tory regime,

This is their phantom factory that they control in cyberspace

For they believe, that we believe, they are the super race!

Eton's Will. 24.12.18

Their institutions go back centuries with many guises, different names,

Both organised and deadly where all things remain the same

They need you now but not for long for the end's not far away

There's a burden they need rid of and that's you, you're in their way.

They have potent brains and function best when the weakest minds believe

And those weak of mind betray the rest and force us all to grieve.

They are carrying out their orders ensuring Eton's will's addressed

But these fools are not idiots, evil looms at their behest.

Their destruction has no measure with allegiances unclear

With a hatred changing daily through a love that's insincere

Discussions are not their remit, their democracy is dead

You gave us a dictatorship when you allowed them in your head!

Seaview Project.   **Hogmanay 2018.**

Let them run wild in their watters

Wi' their ferries that huvnae been built

Nae captains, nae records, nae port yit

But Tory money's backed them tae the hilt.

We could aye lend them The Vital Spark

Wi' Para Handy stood at the helm,

Jeezuz, even the auld Yoker Ferry

Will get tae Oostende before them.

Or how's aboot The Waverley

Wi' a pub crawl doon The Clyde

The last stoap bein' The Broomielaw

Afore we head oot wi' the tide.

They've nae invoice, nae cargo, nae nothin'

Nae ferries, nae ships an' nae boats

But still their reporters keep comin'

Tae take doon corrupted wee notes.

Broon envelopes bulge their back poakits

But there's never a scam tae report

Oh! They'll tell ye the ferries are runnin'

While the dockers still wait fur their port.

Wait! Whit's that ah see in the distance

Home-made canoes pullin' rafts

That's the investment ye get fae The Tories

An' ye still vote for this bundle o' laughs.

Hingin' Fae Sills.   **Hogmanay 2018.**

Noo Ah know that oor country's no' perfect

An' there's still a lot needs tae be done

But we cannae control oor ain future

Until Independence is won.

Ah've had tenement jessies hing fae sills

And gie'in' us a' sorts o' laughs

Ah've hud clerics an' judges walk by mah side

An' ah've heard a' the nutters an' nyaffs

Ah've passed by The Jaikit an' laughed in his face

An' aft questioned if he hud a brain

Ah've seen them beside him, who don't say a word,

Glaikit smiles are a' that remain.

Next year we'll build oan the foundations

That we set up four years ago

Their lies huv come tae fruition

An' much mair they don't want us tae know

So when ye're thinkin' up new resolutions

An' Auld Scotia looks intae yer eyes

Wi' a message regarding her future

It should come as nae great surprise

For as New Year approaches and we bury the last

Fae the ashes a new force will rise

They'll be oot o' their hooses and doon on the streets

Warmin' tae Westminster's demise.

We gied them their chances, they spurned them,

Parity was a' that we asked

But the greed o' Westminster's richest

Meant that wis always too great a task.

Deceit an' corruption wis a' that they hud

An' it's a' they ever can be

An' when they're singin' Auld Lang Syne

They'll be settin' Scotland free.

The Unwashed.   **1.1.19.**

(The politicians sent to Scotland)

Ye send them here unwashed, unclean,

Unshaven, needin' fed

They're the trash that naeb'dy wants

An' like you, they're no' well read.

They haud their hearts within their heids

When siller comes tae mind

Fur treachery is the deadly game

They play tae rob us blind.

The Undesirables.   **1.1.19.**

Can you not see your sons and your daughters

Line the streets that your fathers had paved

They're the dying who live here among us

Sleeping rough 'til we give them their graves.

It's an experience that few of us live through,

A refuge made of paper and board

They are passed by, given our complete silence,

And we're thankful they've just been ignored.

In this cold hearted and feeble existence
Thankful canines share their grotty bed
For inhumanity with all of her riches
Has shown our humanity's dead.

For as they swim in that hopeless great ocean
Sharks prey on the feeblest of minds
And yet we allow them to scour our bins
Then jail them for the scraps that they find.

Squawking seagulls are better protected
Than those we choose to disown
We feed the birds - but the unnoticed -
Will die out there, alone.

They are just some of the many unnoticed
But we don't hear them complain
For we never stop to talk to them
And don't see or feel their pain.

They stare at the night before sleeping
And given up wishing on stars

They've even given up on long lost dreams

And accept just who they are.

Undesired, unwanted and unneeded

They sleep, bundled up, on the floor

While their backs catch the drips from the gutters

Above a carefully guarded old door.

They're the ones we never see

We don't listen to or hear

They're the ones who we all know

The ones who are not here!

My Heart Bleeds.   **1.1.19.**

My heart bleeds for you little England

You're still living a dream that has died

Your bigots still think they've an Empire

And there's no more for them to decide

But this bigotry's making you hated

Yet you won't put these people down

They're burning the cross of the Klan

And you're burning your land to the ground.

They're the Arian race of the Nazi

But you put their leaders in power

And they're selling off every known asset

And your air doesn't even turn sour.

Your queen still hands out gongs for an Empire,

An Empire that doesn't exist

God help me, my friends down in England,

Which part of your history did you miss?

So as you moan of these Lords and their Ladies

Who get your week's wages a day

Accept that you are the culprit

And their wages are making you pay!

Scare me!

Highlight yer contempt, ah dare an' try yer best tae scare me
Fire up yer evil, empty words an' ah'll let yer rhetoric snare ye.

The Unveiling.   **1.1.19.**

You summon your legions to office,

Vengeful, demanding revenge

Who are the traitors and who have they betrayed

And why must you be avenged?

Are you disgraced by contemporary speakers

Who condemn you because you have failed

You can rot in your dungeon of justice

'Til the free flag of Scotland's unveiled.

You have backed yourself into a corner

Imprisoned with no hope of escape

And the country you're holding to ransom

Is rapidly changing her shape.

Numbered are your days of tyrannical rule

And less are the powers you hold

For Scotland no longer gives freely

The key to her being controlled.

My heart bleeds for you, friends in England,

You're still living a dream that has died,

Your bigots still think they've an Empire

And there's no more for them to decide

But this bigotry's making you hated

Yet you won't put these people down

They're burning the cross of the Klan

And you're burning your land to the ground.

They're the Arian race of the Nazi

And you put their leaders in power

But they're selling off every known asset

And your air doesn't even turn sour.

Your queen hands out gongs for an Empire,

An Empire that doesn't exist

God help me, my friends down in England,

Which part of your history did you miss?

So as you moan of these Lords and their Ladies

Who get your week's wages each day

You are the culprit who feeds them

And their wages are making you pay!

She comes to your screen every evening

And you believe that she cares

But the lullabies she sings are worthless

She's a killer posing as your au pair.

Our unveiling is just the beginning

Do you yourself not want to be free

They are guilty of treason to all of us,

A pawn is all they'll let you be.

To Whom It May Concern.　　　3.1.19.

(as Ministers change daily).

Dear Sir or maybe Madam, I feel obliged to seek advice

And I thought I'd come straight to you because others aren't so nice,

I would like to start a business but it all seems so complex

But with you there's no collateral, no persuading and no checks.

Presently, I'm not working but I have everything set in place

I have a business plan, a website so you will not be disgraced.

I find your benevolence overwhelming (Oh! And your cut's the going rate)

And by the way, my plan came from, your project
Seaborne Freight!

The Devils' Game.   3.1.19.

The high priestess by the altar stands and mocks the crowd
below

Saying, all our gods are in on this, it's all part of our show,

You played the devils' game with us and took the angel's
share

But the beast you fed has conjured your despair.

You Are Finished.   6.1.19.

I am not an indulgence

You keep for your bed

And it's good I revolt you

And get inside your head

Your time is now over

Then what will you do

For my friends are many,

The curse of the few.

Agincourt and All That Shit.   7.1.19

I had learned of the Romans and the leaders they had

Their emperors and Hadrian's Wall

Of The Iceni and Boudica who fought Roman's might

And how it was her final call

I was told of King Arthur, his round table and Knights

Of Camelot and Merlin's great power

Tintagel, Avalon, Saxons and Kings

All the history I got wasn't ours.

The Viking invasions, The Normans Conquest

And a King's death not true to the facts

The far off Crusading for Christendom

And Saladin's Moorish attacks

I, at last, got The Bruce taking spider's advice

One lesson for just a short while

Before him was Wallace but that wasn't taught,

The same as The Lord of The Isles

Nor The Vikings defeat between Yoker and Largs

The Clearances, lowland or high

The Picts or The Scots, just who they were

And did they disappear or just die!

I learned of Glencoe and the Campbells,

Who murdered the MacDonalds in bed

But not of the man who said their lives must end

It was "Our" King who ordered them dead!

They hid Culloden's great clearance

Of our culture and how we once dressed

The murders, the destruction, the famine

Or the children they raped to impress

Or the fact they deported our people

If they spoke in their native tongue

And how they were beaten, jailed, exiled

With some even known to be hung

Or those forced to meetings that never occurred

But found soldiers with guns there instead

And those with the guts to oppose them

Were locked in, then burned in their beds.

A factor's their cowardly betrayal

With "our" King being let off Scot Free

And the failure of The Damien Project

Was the same King who wanted us on our knees.

I can tell you about our great Empire

And the millions we murdered by race

But I never learned that in a classroom

Or why Churchill was never disgraced.

In World Wars we fought off the Nazis

But we fight them again here today

We see them out there saluting

The British establishment way.

Do these people know of their history?

Maybe their own family died

Yet they fall for that murky confusion

Where clarity's always denied.

They still offer nothing to Scotland

Our history's still hidden away

And the only way we'll find the truth out

Is when we get our Independence one day.

The Hated Elite. 7.1.19.

I was saddened and embarrassed but not too surprised

At the rise of Nazi England there before my very eyes

You crawled into that dark place you call the UK

You crawled back to enjoy their complete disarray

You crawled under their covers and pretend nothing's wrong

Convince yourself, singing, their wee ruling song.

The waves you once ruled are now your barricade

And they say it's the best thing that they ever made

But it's built of contempt with a dash of their hate

Thrown together by racists where they, The Fascists, dictate.

They'll tell you the UK and England's the same

But the wiser among you know who's just to blame

They'll say it's your flag but it's not England's own

It's belongs to elitists and the queen on your throne.

You have nothing in common, they're masters, you're slaves

You're only some fodder they want for their graves.

They offer you nothing but they keep it discreet

Their hands don't get dirty, they are the elite

What are you scared of, you're ruled by the deranged,

Realise your dreams and demand England's change.

Another Un-Bloody Civil War.   10.1.19.

The media's gone into meltdown

We're at war again. Hurrah!

Get ready, get yer best gear on

Battle statins men. Hurrah!

All you lovely ladies

Jist make yersels look good

For tomorrow at the crack o' dawn

We descend on Holyrood!

The General's called us a' tae arms

Sir Alex, take a bow

Yon Evans seeks revenge again

The stupid bloody cow!

Westminster's reinforced her purse

So here she will remain

Lead us now Sir Alex

And for The Record, show disdain.

Yon Evans is a devious thing

But her mind that's full o' rage

Her guard is down, now let us go,

Move forward wi' oor sage

The Mail had delivered warring notes

Biased liars lined oor streets

And the buses up fae London

Revved up for their retreat

Their insatiable thirst for blood was quelled

When Evans seemed tae swoon

She wis hit square wi' loveheart

An' the wummin' jist fell doon.

Love hud conquered hate again

An' Sir Alex, aye the gent

Watched the buses then return

Tae their holding bay in Kent.

The Union papers next, day, read

That we attacked them first

A loveheart's a' it seems tae take

Tae quench their bloody thirst.

Towards Independence.   10.1.19.

I don't need the props of false friends and flags

I am much stronger than you

I don't need decisions made on my behalf

I determine my own points of view

My love is a strength you never will have

Including my Scottish resolve

And can't wait for the day like most in this land

When this outdated Union's dissolved.

I am proud I can stand on my own two feet

Without the help of aides

I am proud my head is high when I walk

I can, through the judgements I've made

I suffer indifference with balance of mind

And address them without any fear

The pride of my nation is here, inside me

And I know that my conscience is clear.

But for those who need propped up by false friends and flags

You've denied belief in your head

Without honour there's no point in living

Your belief is their greatest dread.

The Road to Independence.   10.1.19.

The road to Independence gets shorter every day,

Only lengthened by the fear they feel, as the lie in disarray,

Tyrants and usurpers rise but, eventually, they will fall

So rise and take what's rightfully yours and answer Scotland's call.

Fae Wishy Tae The Boag.   10.1.19.

Alarm bells ring in The Horseshoe Bar an' four drinks later we a' get barred

And so do those who nodded to say Hi

Wi' Union flags and British queens the wee boss wummin
wis obscene

She'd noticed Jackie's wristband sayin' AYE!

Ah wis gauny say ye're being absurd but big Will said, Sssh!
Not a word

And so we headed out tae huv a night

It wis Denholm's or The Alpen Lodge, so long as we wurr
oot o' Dodge

It wis freezin' but these stars were shinin' bright.

Noo they've watches smothered in curry sauce, these Indy

girls don't give a toss

That's whit happens when ye hit The Blue Lagoon

Fae heid tae toe they're black n' blue! How'd that happen?

Ah've nae clue

As half a Russian met his ain high noon!

They tell me now they they're quite bereft but at least

they've got some kitty left

A' they want tae dae is huv some fun

Fae Wishy and the Boag they came an' ah' no sayin' any
names

But efter nights wi' them ah'm always done!

None of Us Know. 13.1.19.

Must we return to the stories they told long ago

To a place in the past that none of us know

Written by "authors" who never came here

Who showed through their hatred, words written in fear.

We were the comedic laughter in all England's plays

We were cannibals, savages, all based on hearsay,

We feasted on flesh from the maiden's fresh breasts

And on the buttocks of shepherds, to which all Europe attests

From the Greeks to the Dutch to the great absentees

This was the Scotland which those authors decreed,

In their futile arrangement we are still put on show

In some monotonous wilderness, we are still seen the foe

They still mock our existence and still rob from our land,

Nothing's upfront, it is all underhand.

Their indulgence in greed will not wane nor decline

And nor will that thirst to fake their Scottish bloodline

Where pretence is a virtue and opens doors to success

And where their betrayal of Scotland can best be expressed.

The Rags An' A' Their Writings.   **14.1.19.**

The panicked anguish in their words are hastily thrown at us

Their scattered letters thrown doon, they scramble oot their words

Yon Massie hings by tattered threads as his London puppeteers

Dance him like a like a lunatic wi' their unimpeded smears.

He asks us tae believe his words yet he writes wi' nae belief

Another London siller man who applauds his country's grief

For who would take a pride in words that go against yer ain

The disrespect he shows tae us is as much as their disdain.

The Scotsman ance so freely read now lies in deathly throes

And its swansong just a whimper as we watch her final shows

For nothin's ever looked at, their diggin' null and void

An' when we question whit they write, we are the paranoid

But it's destined for a bonfire where false stories go tae die

And wi' it a' the journalists, doomed for a' their lies

But this mans no' the only ane who'd see us on oor erse

But when oor Independence comes, there'll be ane great paper hearse.

The Enemy At The Front Door.   15.1.19.

The blood of this Union has stained many hands

And coloured the rivers that flow through our lands

We're at peace but the killings go on as before

As thousands are dying behind their front door.

They're dying of hunger not bombed by a shell,

They're taking their own lives to resign from their hell

But the bombs from Westminster keep raining down

They're still killing our people and endorsed by the Crown.

Well An' Truly Pumped.   **15.1.19.**

Pumped again, humped again but we expected nothing less

Get aff your knees an' resign ya swine, yer a catastrophic mess

Truth's reflection's never lied and comes wi' a vivid guarantee

An' ye've avoided every mirror, scared of whit yer eyes will see.

Ye're hated here, as Thatcher wis, but ah think that you're the worst

Contempt of court wis jist the start an' noo yer bubble's finally burst

Yer arrogance was paramount an' yer defeat wis justified

Ye were well an' truly telt the night wi' a' those cretins by yer side

Ye caused the worst defeat in history, that is poetry tae oor ears

Maybe noo we'll get a government, an' ane we vote fur here!

Mundell SS. 16.1.19.

Sing for your supper, Aye! You! With the specs

Is there anything at all that you haven't wrecked?

You whimpering weasel, you slovenly slob

We pay you in Scotland to do one simple job,

That's to look after your country, you snivelling creep

But you're so far up her arse you're asleep.

You panic and squeal like a true autocrat

Siding with pals in your wee coup d'état

Deserting your country like the lowlife you are

Wandering through Scotland like a political star

But that fortified castle with your three thousand men

Will be sent back to London, signed off by a pen

For you've only awakened by all your mistrust

Those who believed you and gave you their trust.

Scotophobia. 16.1.19.

One looks like a nonce and we know one's a ponce

And they both like to baulk when the SNP talks

One combs his pet hedgehog, one snacks on his beard

And the party they black out's the one that is feared!

They know they'll be sheltered by their media boss

A schemer complicit to gain Scotland's loss

They can't bear to say a nation's party by name

They just cut them off then degrade and defame.

Scotophobia's demanded where surrealism reigns

They turn back to a House full of spoilt brats and weans

This programme presenter would like us all brought to
heel

As he dreams of his ermine and how that must feel.

The mad bearded traitor has that same sense of grandeur

When the snacks from his beard will be left to the poor

They're delusional people who will never back down

They're after their Lordships, bestowed by their Crown.

The Firing Gun.   17.1.19.

You just wouldn't listen, you always know best

But you're trapped in a Brexit that's all your own mess

We'll stay in Europe while we leave the UK

It's what Scotland wants, not what Westminster says,

I've a mandate to use, Scotland's ready to fight

The starting gun's polished and you're in my sights

And I've a nice little cartridge, our Saint Andrew's Cross

My muscles are flexed, I'll show you who's the boss!

Smoke and Mirrors.   18.1.19.

Do you stare into your own eyes

And see another self on show

Or do you see a truthful person

One you do not know

Or do you stare into another's eyes

And ponder at the sight

Or does truth throw her reflection

Reeling at your plight?

You avoid the mirror, knowingly,

It bears no guarantee

For in reflection is a truth

Which you refuse to see.

Truth is never easy

When you confront it face to face

But the mirror's face can never lie

It is you who are misplaced.

YES Glasgow North West's Quiz Night.

Big Joe and his good lady, Hayley,

Presented our Quiz here tonight

Where Stewards' Enquiries were welcomed

If their answers were deemed not quite right.

As the mob bayed for blood from their tables

From these, normally, mild mannered men,

All was solved by a quick search through Google

And these peacemakers returned once again.

But others then roared from their corners

And some even rose to their feet

It resembled the Halls of Westminster

Like a rabble confronting defeat

Our presenters often cried Order

And in the end, their efforts were praised

It was a night where the banter was endless

With more than three hundred quid raised.

The blonde, blue-eyed lady from Scotstoun,

Sporting the shirt of Yes Glasgow North West

Then presented, to the winners, their trophy

Partick's locals had conquered our best.

As they left, we applauded our victors,

All Yessers who vowed to be back

And one final thank you to The Smiddy

Thanks to you all for the craic.

This Quiz Night had auctions and raffles

Where many a drink was consumed

But I fear there'll be some this bright morning

Who are still spinning around in their rooms!

Alex And YES.   24.1.19.

To me it's a smear by The Great British State

He's the threat to The Union and the man they all hate

They want him put down, banged up, put him jail

And hope that without him, Independence will fail.

We've read all the smears and we've heard their reports

He's been to the Police and we've seen him leave court

He's been charged but not guilty, his innocence stands,

He has still to be tried by the laws of his land.

He's been charged with sex crimes which he strongly refutes

They're afraid of his power and his great attributes

But don't let them distract you, there is no compromise,

And no matter what happens, keep your eyes on the prize.

Independence is coming, we have strengthened resolve

We will demand Independence and this Union dissolved

For YES is much bigger than one name or one man

YES is the voice of our people, our land.

The Parcel's Still Here. 25.1.19.

The parcel's still here celebrating yer songs

While takin' the siller you scorned

They bow tae auld England in the great London ha's

Hopin' tae be ermine adorned

They fill up plush rooms wi' their tartan an' pipes

A' hypocrites bidin' their time

Dancin' an' drinkin' tae the words o' The Bard

While plottin' their great Scottish crime.

Wi' false admiration they get up an' speak

Stirrin' false hearts wi' their quotes

The Union's alive wi' these traitors

Who're still tuggin' at the tails o' Lords' coats.

The pride o' oor nation's wasted on them

And we burden oorsels wi' their shame

But they're clingin' on tae a dream o' the past

Oor Scotland will soon be reclaimed.

The Mandate.   4.2.19

Oh! You hypocritical bastards, for once fight Scotland's fight

The mandate for Independence is there and to use it is our right.

When Scotland's government called on you to pass a budget for all Scots

You held them up to ransom but unlike you they can't be bought!

Your contempt is not unnoticed, you want Scotland to stand still

Or further fall into decline as you bow to London's will

Again, you've gone against the people with your refusal to discuss

A budget meant for every Scot was met with your disgust.

When London's crime lords beckon, you shuffle to their door

On your skint knees with your worn out tongues showing us you're only whores

You negotiate on their behalf with blackmail foremost in your mind

You have no love for Scotland, you or your London kind!

You've shown yourselves to Scotland as the quislings we all thought

You have bowed again to London and yet you call yourself a Scot!

Our Time.   4.2.19.

They've an arrogance enthused by their own self belief

Stealing our honesty to replace it with grief

They're political bankers with an no assumed name

And the theft of these countries is, to them, all a game

These people are bankers and you feed their accounts

You're the key to investment where every deal counts

These "Politicians for People" is just one of their acts,

Did you vote to be poorer while they pay no tax

And stealing your pensions was just their idea of fun,

Name them and jail them for the wrongs they have done.

They're killing the poor and filled up paupers' graves

Another statistic transferred and then saved

They bargained this Brexit for themselves and not you

But you jumped on their bandwagon, it was something to do

There's no money left but there's money for bribes

And always for wars to which they eternally prescribe

But the pompous and righteous with their Empirical grit

Want Eire to join them and deal with their Brexit shit

These retards who rule us still demand without power

Forgetting the famine, the murders, their bloodthirsty hours

The innocent slaughters, Churchill's bold Black'n'tans

This is still fresh in the minds of these people, their land.

The world has moved on but it's left England behind

They're still propping up leaders who've no thought for mankind

And while the world looks on and shakes a forsaken head

The UK Government maestros just keep pushing ahead

With no thought for their people, their jobs or their rights,

The time is now for Scotland to push our Independence fight.

Westminster's English MPs.   4.2.19.

They tell us to Fuck Off quite proudly, sincerely

Then, Piece of Shit, mumbled, distinctly and clearly

While a young woman fighting for all women's rights

Is a whore, a slut, an ugly cunt, is that right?

When you look at our Mairi, tell me what do you see?

I see a reflection of what we should all aim to be

She has command of a language that speaks for us all

Impassioned yet simple that will see your downfall.

She asks for the truth but none's to be found

They are hidden in files deep down underground

But you know where they are, you just cannot tell

If you did you'd be killed or your life made a hell.

A Union of Equals, aww for fuck's sake get real

They're all robbing bastards and Scotland's their steal

When Ian Blackford stands up, their leaders stand and walk by

His voice, again, is unheard, then told, Go Back to Skye.

Laborious Labour.   5.2.19.

For decades they fed us their bullshit,

Knowing Scotland was their greatest prize

English Labour has no place in our country,

It's here their democracy dies

We're abhorred by their ignorant leader

This messiah could not raise a smile

He's another Keir Hardie would banish

Just another of "that" rank and file.

His reality's a meagre distraction

As the truth is held back for the few

And the lies that are fed to the many

Are all part of their Great British coup.

This austere boring voice that he speaks with

Is revered by the handful that's left

But when the starkest of truths are considered

It shows Labour's a party bereft.

His disciples cajoling in Holyrood

Have a Judas devoid of all sense

They've no ambition, no plan, it's all theatre

And their enactment is all a pretence.

And they wonder why membership plummet,

Now a phone box is ample in size

To address the remnants of Labour,

The party who back Tory lies.

New Winds of War.   6.2.19.

The blood of our killings has stained many hands

And coloured the rivers that flowed through our lands

We're at peace but the killings go on as before

When will we stand up and fight back in this war!

The winds carry new deaths with no sign of relief

They're still chilling our homes which are laden with grief

There is no consolation for a lover who's gone

When the bleakest of days start with blackest of dawns.

Some mourn for their children, their child has no age,

They'll always be babies which the years cannot gauge

And those tears turn to rivers, running faster each day,

And the blood keeps on coming, it won't wash away.

Our people are starving and have no human rights

They're huddled in corners, left with no will to fight

Destitute, hungry in some makeshift old den

They're wiped out of existence by a cruel system's pen.

To the system they're nothing, they're just struck off a list

Where they're not even counted so will never be missed!

What's the cost to our country, our people, our land

When this Union is measured by the blood on their hands.

Ross "Touchy" Thomson.   **8.2.19.**

Who are these perverted folk who fondle strangers like they're whores

Hanging onto bulging arses to break their falls to bar-room floors

No he's embarrassed for his poor family but his notoriety grows

Falling drunk with flailing hands, (stuffing Charlie up his nose?)

Fondling fanciable arses, unconscious where his hands should be

And his desperate pleas of innocence are no more than just a plea.

He was steaming drunk in Westminster how would he

know what went on?

He'd been asked to leave the bar three times, the man was absolutely gone

But as he recuperates today, he'll be pleased he's hit the headline's news

And we all know that glaikit look and even worse, his glaikit views.

On Monday, he'll be walking, back through Westminster's doors

And he'll take it out on Scotland, we are all Ross Thomson's whores!

Share and Shoot!   12.2.19.

Stop buying their papers, they're Scotland's disgrace

You're buying them bullets to shoot **you** in the face

They need your shares to feed you their lies

And as their right wing rag sales drop their staff numbers rise.

They are wimps taking wages from the rich upper class

To ensure we stay down and that we shall not pass

They've amassed a paid army and they're all watching you

You're their sworn enemy as you've got your own view.

They're fond of a headline and their mock Indy polls

But they seem to win nothing and that tears out their souls

We now can see through them, they are shocked but that's tough

Scotland's people once listened but now we've all had enough!

The Real Enemy.   **13.2.19.**

The angry hordes don battle dress

To show pathetic joyful hate

Standing tall with chests puffed out,

As one, they seal our fate.

They vilify, condemn and trounce

And fight on through defeats

They'll conquer countries, continents

Yet never leave their seats

And as they roll out tanks and guns

From the comfort of their bench

These warlords want lethality

And send you smugly to your trench.

Their flippant words condemn us all

Bared with a corporate smile

It's a circumstance enforced on all

In that pompous Tory style.

Contempt!   13.2.19.

Oh Scotland! how you're treated

And the contempt in which you're held

You stand to question all that's wrong

But with the English axe you're felled

They allow the paedos, rapists

And the touchy, feely hands

To roam around their bars at night

But Scottish truths are banned!

Scotch Labour. 14.2.19.

Scotch Labour, Scottish Labour

None o' ye exist

Yir rid rose turned tae royal blue

When the Tory arse wis kissed

But may ye send each other Valentine

Wi' the words ye baith deserve

For we know the bed ye share so much

Is where yer treachery is served.

Dreamers. 16.2.19.

Do you walk with your heart in a basket

Hoping someone will kindle its fire

Or do you have faith in your own expectations

With dreams to which you can aspire?

We are one of the richest of nations

With a third world right in our midst

And while the richest enjoy life with fervour

The dreams of the poor are dismissed.

When we stand over friends in the cemetery

All in black with heads bowed to mourn

We don't think of the countless of others

Who lie in their graves marked, unknown!

These early homes built by depravity

The last home of the oppressed

Even dreams are dictated by wealth here

They are laid with their last dream to rest.

Are dreams only there for the richest

Have they made dreams for the poorest exempt,

When people say, you are a dreamer,

I ask them, have you never dreamt?

Kirsty Blackman.   20.2.19.
(The Smiley One).

Like her hair this lady's short but with a heart that's quite immense

And proud of where she comes from, of that, there's no pretence

If you don't know this lady then I wonder where you've been,

You can find her by the Northern lights, way up in Aberdeen.

And she'll always talk up Scotland as her perfect diction states

Whilst talking down this Union which we know's in dire straits.

She flicks a scarf around her neck and dons her trademark smile

And talks outside a parliament with her usual craft and

Guile

But condemned before she even speaks she encounters them with grace

By responding with an honest voice and a great big smiling face.

She knows we're right behind her and no matter how they goad

We'll be walking down together on our Independence Road.

Sunken Ships to Independence.   20.2.19.

Look who's sailing down the river

Look who's heading out to sea

Corporate convoys filled with bankers

With holes in every hull we see.

Yes, they're sailing from our waters

With all our riches safe onboard

Billionaires with foreign passports

Sailing with their stolen hoard

But look! Their ships are sinking slowly

They're now below the water line

No-one heeds the poor man's warnings

Tory chaos is refined!

Yes we stand here on the shoreline

Watching as their ships go down

Dinghies left behind can't save them

Or their precious golden crowns.

Will we gather at their graveside

I don't think so, said The Scots

With open arms we tried to save them

But they'd no time for foreign thoughts.

Now the sea is calm and settled

There are no battles left to fight

All that's left is Independence

Which Scotland sees as Scotland's right.

An Inconvenient Marriage.   8.3.19.

We wed out of convenience without love or blissful airs

I shared with her my riches then watched my land stripped bare,

She took that fertile mind of mine 'til all control was hers

Then fed me lies 'til I believed that loneliness is worse

And that prayer was not the answer as god was on her side

And each Sunday she reminds him with all her evil pride.

Though words are shunned, she heeds them, to keep for later use

And no doubt I'll feel her iron wrath in this marriage of abuse.

The years went by and life grew hard, much harder than before

And no matter what I gave to her she always wanted more

But more was never near enough and thought she earned some recompense

God, I questioned why we really wed but knew it all was just pretence.

She curses me beneath her breath, berating me at every turn

I feel not hurt but rage towards her and this once warm heart now burns.

My partner now holds me a slave, that my words will not be heard

And divorce, I cannot mention, as each time it's just deferred.

The feeble mind's a lonely place where nothing is arranged

Sanest thoughts can be displaced with the simplest thoughts deranged

When I stand I'm told to sit, shut up, be silent with my plea

And bound to some far flung bench where no-one speaks for me,

Our vows were never honoured, no loving kiss e'er sealed

This inconvenient marriage still has wounds that never healed.

Permission. 11.2.19.

There's a right Royal Palace in London

That's falling apart at the seams

It's a place where the guilty are many

And dash all our hopes and our dreams,

They tell me they've qualifications

They're learned and know what they do

But the only reason they're in there

Is they were sent down there by The Broo!

In this palace of posh boys and paedos

Where your friends are not what you think

They're thinking ahead to the nightlife

When some get too touchy with drink,

The prices in there are quite normal

Much more than I say of some guests

But there's one who is more than familiar

And that's Aberdeen's poshest sex pest.

They'll lead you to their devastation

Every promise they'll tell you they'll keep

But we know that they'll never deliver

They're the ones who gave us, talk is cheap,

They've travelled the world ten times over

Flashing their honorary degrees,

To every nation they bow or they curtsey

Then tell Scotland to get on its knees.

They come here indignant and pompous

With an arrogance no-one believes

And still acting as though they're an Empire

But it's only what the futile perceive,

This Act of Union is broken

But some think they are the licensee

We do not need Westminster's permission

Our sovereignty will see Scotland free.

My Presence.   **14.3.19.**

This hall is almost empty, the government has withdrawn

They do not wish my presence but will notice when I'm gone

I'm surrounded by a silence yet still cut the atmosphere

Where ugly allies stare with eyes, eyes I see full of fear.

Why do the many walk away, disrespecting what I'm due

Why do they hiss and jeer and diss the words of those so few

Is the truth so hard for them to bear that contempt is all they serve

And those Scots who sit beside them think we get what we deserve.

In a past life that was treason but their betrayal is now a skill

Where constituents thoughts are swept aside and branded overkill

Yet they rest with their impunity tattooed glibly on their heads

With deceptive speeches paramount, at the fore of all that's said,

These parasites feed off apathy and will not listen to my voice

They can empty halls, ignore me but Scotland has another choice.

Silencers. **21.3.19.**

We have played the role of silencers

With complicit hearts and minds

We let ourselves be victors

With our history redefined

For victors always write the words

Where truth is often lost

Our silence has caused suffering

And made sure we bore the cost

But we deserve no pity

Scots are good at going for gold,

We are only traitors to ourselves

When we trade in our souls.

A Beautiful Heart and Mind. **27.3.19.**
(A poem written for my friend, Donna Babbington).

Her eyes shone through a shining heart that warmed up
the Glasgow air

And there, by a cold stall smiling, she sold her Scottish
wares,

Her hair gleamed like a silver sun, her face, so fresh, alive

She has words that must be heard by all if nature's to survive.

By the streams she walked passed as a child are still captured in her eyes,

The walks through her enchanted woods grasp every breathless sigh

By flora, fauna, burnished leaves that decorate the soil she scours

For the insignificants, we forget, who adorn our trees and flowers.

When the purest heart sheds a tear, and falls from the fairest face,

Down from eyes that once held smiles then fall to another place

It's a sadness very few can see and, sadly, fewer hearts can feel,

And though words conveyed may be ignored, they must never be concealed.

With every snap she captures, more tears drop from her heart

As words pour from a troubled mind that sees her world being ripped apart

Her course is that where nature leads, each path captured by her lens

But how beautiful her mind must be with nature such a friend.

Wrapped in Freedom's Chains.   21.3.19.

I want to see my country free and never again be sold

And those who're here from foreign lands with stories still untold

Can stand upright beside us and make our nation great

And leave behind the great deception they call The British State.

It's a sordid place where nothing's changed and nothing gets resolved

How can Scotland progress when they've still not evolved?

Our liberty lies with sovereignty, it is us who wield the powers

Our people's voice must now be heard and take back what is ours.

They build their walls to watch us fall built by dictatorial rule

And while we rise against them, they're backed by the British fool.

Our children are abandoned, their freedom's been curtailed

And though I have travelled far and wide, our children have been failed.

Our scathing attacks on their uselessness, are unreserved and justified

They have lied to you, lied to themselves and spoken with a fascist's pride

Their leader stood up yesterday and deflected all and any blame

She has wrapped us all in Freedom's chains, she is England's shame.

Evasions. 8/4/19.

We dream and then we live that dream but, alas, without belief

But they, they stand and pronounce their pride then steal like a common street thief,

They're all up for auction where high interest wins with their conscience included for hire,

Their limitless wealth is progressed by their crimes and the banks give them all they desire.

These financial wizards indulge in themselves and this in itself is their curse,

They're the real refugees who have no need or care, they're allied to none but their purse,

Theirs is a world where they make the rules or finance the criminals who do,

Theirs is a wilderness where no loyalty's asked, robbing us then bidding adieu!

They are the embodiment of this great British state and corrupt as any known power,

They brandish their tongues and deny any wrong but their words are what you devour,

With all feelings excluded, their souls bear no sin and they don't care if borders exist,

Avoidance, evasion, no tax is paid here, their havens are Britain's abyss.

Accession.   13.4.19.

Who will accede the Tory throne when so many share their
hate,

Which unthinking Eton, Oxbridge head could run The
British State

When uncontrollable incompetence is the eejit's foremost
trait?

There are so many here to choose from, each one the devil
incarnate!

Kirstene Hair.   14.4.19.

She eloquently stands up to speak
As if butter wouldn't melt

But before she sits back down again
She gets well and truly Telt!

Behind the pristine painted face
Is a wit devoid of charm

A woman who'd deny her dad
The wealth due for his farm

And below that mane of shining blonde
Is a force that seeks out fame

But no-one's ever told her
That her brain has been reclaimed.

I hear the echoes multiply
Through a rattling hollow head

A flummoxed look and vacant eyes
Belie the words she's fed

You see in her face bewilderment,
Puzzlement laced with awe

Then logically reach your conclusion,
This woman knows nothing at a'!

Who catapulted her to power
And what right has she to fame

If her scripts were not pre-written
I'm sure she'd struggle with her name!

Very Well Hidden Talents.   **22.3.19.**

Hark! The Tory talisman, she begs us hear her once again,

Fumbling on her foreign stage, where she's still to find a friend,

She says, I am tired, nay, exhausted exclaims this nauseous, trembling wreck

Slithering like a poisoned snake with a noose around its neck.

The fault is yours and yours alone, I pronounce myself exempt

It is they, those gods of Westminster, who show me nothing but contempt

Just because I am the leader in this circus full of clowns

They will say the fault is mine and that I have let you down.

This pathetic figure on her own, this living, human gaffe

Holds out to us her innocence as the world around us laughs

This conundrum who walks on stilts, slightly drugged yet fully dazed

And demands the only words we heed should be the words of Theresa May's!

Where The Wild Thistle Grows.   **20.4.19.**

I see them proudly satisfied

Wearing tags of, born to lose

But they rejoice in having nothing

For it's a blinded choice they choose

Yet there's a pride in their contentment

And they truly feel they're blest

While the Union that they idolise

Is the one keeping them oppressed.

They're enveloped in a history

That is seldom criticised

They read it without question

Not knowing they're the ones despised

They celebrate their victors

While they see the slain, slaves

Not realising it was their ancestors

Who were thrown in those graves.

The stories of these battlefields

Are in the wind that blows

Swirling round the death and heartache

Where the wild thistle grows

Those barren moors lie empty now

Rugged and untamed

And below them lie the unknown Scots

They are hidden like our history

The ones they never taught,

Cultivated by the British State

And groomed by treacherous Scot

We must challenge every learned word

Our hand must write our fate

Or cower in surrender

And be devoured by the State.

I would like to end with this poem I wrote on our most famous poet, Rabbie Burns.

The Man o' Words.   **12.3.19.**

He wrapped himsel' in Scotland

Fought the fight that others craved

An' cursed this heartless Union

An' those who made us slaves,

Tae the man who gied us honest words

This man who tilled his field

Tae the man who never gied a damn

Tae the man who widnae yield.

He enriched the poor wi' painted words

An' brought tae life their dreams

Wi' ghouls an' ghosts an' witches

An' luve by bonnie streams,

Tae the man we know as Rabbie

Who felt their honest pain

A' sculpted oot in giant bronze

Wi' a vista a' his ain.

No' only are ye cast in bronze

Ye're cast in Scottish hearts

And the usurpers that ye wrote of

Ripped oor nation wide apart,

Tae the man who's up there lookin' doon

We can feel yer earthly gaze

Tae a man unlike nae other,

Quite deservin' o' oor praise.

Tae the man who gave us a' he had

Whose words were aft unkind

Tae a Scottish bard wi' a Scottish heart

And his independent mind.

Thank you so much for your ongoing support, encouragement and I hope you enjoy your book.

Aye yours,

Saor Alba gu Brath

Paul.

Poem.   **Page.**

Printed in Great Britain
by Amazon

59580492R10172